RAINFORESTS

Other Books in the At Issue Series:

RAINFORESTS

David Bender, *Publisher*
Bruno Leone, *Executive Editor*

Brenda Stalcup, *Managing Editor*
Scott Barbour, *Series Editor*

Charles P. Cozic, *Book Editor*

An Opposing Viewpoints® Series

Greenhaven Press, Inc.
San Diego, California

Library of Congress Cataloging-in-Publication Data

Rainforests / Charles P. Cozic, book editor.
    p.   cm. — (At issue)
    Includes bibliographical references and index.
    ISBN 1-56510-694-6 (pbk. : alk. paper). — ISBN 1-56510-695-4
(lib. bdg. : alk. paper)
    1. Rainforest conservation. 2. Deforestation. 3. Logging—
Environmental aspects. I. Cozic, Charles P., 1957– . II. Series:
At issue (San Diego, Calif.)
SD411.R34   1998
333.75—dc21   97-38571
                                                              CIP

© 1998 by Greenhaven Press, Inc., PO Box 289009,
San Diego, CA 92198-9009

Printed in the U.S.A.

Table of Contents

Introduction

Rainforests, located in both tropical and temperate climate zones, are dense forests that receive heavy rainfall; those in the tropics receive more than seventy inches per year. Considered by many experts to be Earth's most precious ecosystems, tropical rainforests constitute approximately 7 percent of the planet's land mass—primarily in Africa, Southeast Asia, and Latin America—and provide habitats to more than half of all the earth's plant and animal species. In addition, tropical rainforests supply food, fuel, jobs, medicine, hardwood for products such as home furnishings, and shelter to much of the world's human population. These areas also help to regulate local temperatures, the exchange of atmospheric gases, and the global climate.

The United Nations Food and Agriculture Organization (FAO) reported in 1991 that the tropical forests were being depleted at a rate of 0.9 percent annually. The primary causes of forest loss are clearcutting by commercial loggers and slashing and burning by local farmers to clear land for growing crops and grazing livestock. According to the Rainforest Action Network, "If deforestation continues at current rates, scientists estimate nearly 80–90 percent of tropical rainforest ecosystems will be destroyed by the year 2020."

Many experts and scientists theorize that unabated rainforest depletion will cause long-term—and possibly irreversible—ecological damage. Perhaps the gravest concern surrounds the potential loss of biodiversity. A large proportion of the world's plant and animal species are found in the rainforests, and many could become extinct as the forests are depleted. Conservationist Norman Myers estimates that the extinction of a single plant species could eventually contribute to the death of up to thirty animal species—animals that depend for food either on the plant itself or those insects and animals that live on or near the plant. Besides adversely affecting the environment, this loss of species could impact human health; numerous rainforest species contain chemicals that could potentially serve as ingredients for new drugs to combat AIDS, cancer, and other diseases.

Another threat from rainforest loss, according to many scientists, is its effect on the climate. The United Nations, for example, reports that the clearing of rainforests is responsible for the production of nearly 20 percent of the earth's carbon dioxide, 40 percent of methane, and 25 to 30 percent of nitrous oxide. Many experts theorize that these gases, which are released by the cutting and burning of trees, contribute to global warming by trapping heat in the atmosphere. Computer models also suggest that if rainforests are transformed to grassland, rainfall dramatically decreases and temperatures increase, thus extending dry seasons.

A more direct consequence of tropical deforestation, commentators maintain, involves the displacement of indigenous peoples and entire communities. In the Brazilian Amazon basin and elsewhere, encroachment by loggers, farmers, and miners has forced many indigenous inhabitants to abandon their homes and lands. Observers note that not only have millions of forest acres been denuded, but thousands of miles of roads have been constructed, increasing expansion into indigenous peoples' unspoiled territory. In addition, deforestation results in soil erosion, flooding, and the siltation of rivers and streams—all of which threaten forest dwellers' ability to live off the land.

However, experts disagree about the extent and long-term effects of rainforest loss. According to tropical forestry expert Ariel Lugo, "Only about half of the virgin tropical forests being cut annually are lost; the rest simply become secondary forests and are still good wildlife habitat." Timothy J. Synnott, executive director of the Forestry Stewardship Council, adds, "A forest that has been logged, even carelessly, can usually yield another harvest later on. Many tropical forests, especially in West Africa and tropical America, continue to produce timber after having been selectively logged several times."

Environmentalists, governments, and trade groups seek to preserve virgin rainforests through agricultural practices, commercial procedures, and conservation. In the Brazilian Amazon, according to the U.S. Department of Agriculture, such efforts have helped reduce rainforest loss to 0.3 percent annually, "with even lower rates of loss probable as Brazilians become more affluent and environmentally sensitive."

One popular conservation approach is the establishment of tree plantations, which help meet consumer demand for tropical wood as well as reduce the need to clearcut virgin rainforests. In Africa, Southeast Asia, and Latin America, numerous plantations are successfully producing hardwood trees—primarily mahogany and teak—and plantation acreage is growing rapidly. According to the FAO, "The area of plantations in developing countries alone doubled from 40 million ha [hectares] in 1980 to more than 80 million ha in 1995."

Many governments have granted protected status to rainforest areas, converting them to national parks and reserves, some of which are now devoted to the preservation and cataloguing of species. In response to pressure from environmental groups and government estimates that deforestation had increased 33 percent between 1991 and 1994, Brazil's National Congress in 1996 placed a two-year moratorium on new logging of mahogany, the Amazon region's most valuable tree. Brazil's president also introduced a measure to reduce farming and ranching activities that cause deforestation. One proposed strategy calls for governments to encourage livestock farmers to convert unproductive pastures to rainforests.

In addition to environmentalists and officials, timber industries also proclaim a desire to conserve rainforests. Although timber companies seek profits from the harvesting of mahogany and other tropical trees, it is also in their interest to maintain abundant supplies of these trees in order to remain competitive. As the International Wood Products Association writes, "Quite simply, no trees = no wood = no industry." According to many wood industry experts, loggers aim to imitate as closely as possible the natural processes that affect the growth and loss of rainforest trees.

The attempt to preserve rainforests will be a challenging endeavor in the coming decades. One potential obstacle involves balancing the interests of environmentalists, rainforest inhabitants, and others who demand protection for rainforests with the commercial interests of farmers, loggers, and others who want to clear rainforest land. Rainforest loss and preservation are among the issues discussed and debated in *At Issue: Rainforests*.

1

Multiple Factors Cause Rainforest Loss

John Vandermeer and Ivette Perfecto

John Vandermeer, a professor of biology at the University of Michigan in Ann Arbor, and Ivette Perfecto, an associate professor at the university's School of Natural Resources and the Environment, are the authors of Breakfast of Biodiversity: The Truth About Rain Forest Destruction.

No single factor is responsible for rainforest loss. A combination of causes—including logging, agricultural practices, government policies, and global economic forces—are intricately connected in a "web of causality." In their efforts to conserve the forests, activists must avoid focusing on any one cause of rainforest depletion and must instead address this entire web. Such an approach will require them to link their attempts to conserve the rainforests with the larger effort to secure social justice for the people who live in and around the forests.

The buzz is unmistakable. A huge chain saw cuts effortlessly through the wood of a beautiful rain forest tree, slicing up the trunk it has just felled into smaller bits to be taken away on giant lumber trucks. That image is fixed in our minds. It drives us to the same distraction it has driven so many before us. The rain forests are physically beautiful and contain the vast majority of our relatives on this planet. What sort of person would not be haunted by the sound of chain saws decimating them?

Yet another image is equally haunting. The bulldozed wooden shack, formerly the home of a poor family, constantly reminds us that lives as well as logs are being cut in most areas of tropical rain forests. Hungry children wander among the stumps of once majestic rain forest trees. Their mother cooks over an open fire, and their father fights the onslaught of weeds that continually threaten to choke out the crops the family needs for next year's food. All live in fear that the bulldozers will come again to destroy their present home. What sort of person would not be haunted by the existence of such poverty in a world of plenty?

But for us the power of these two images lies in the way they are con-

From John Vandermeer and Ivette Perfecto, "Rethinking Rain Forests," *Institute for Food and Development Policy Backgrounder*, Summer 1995. Reprinted with permission.

nected, a fact we are reminded of every morning we slice up bananas on our breakfast cereal. The banana cannot be grown in the United States, yet it is one of the most popular fruits here. As we all know, it is produced in the world's tropical regions, usually in the same areas where rain forests have flourished in the past. The link between the decimated forest and the hungry children is the banana. That is why it is so easy, as we slice up a banana in Michigan, for our thoughts to wander to the image of the chain saw slicing up the rain forest trees and the children who view the banana as a staple food rather than a luxury.

The majority of life on earth lives in the rain forest. Close to 80% of the terrestrial species of animals and plants are to be found there. And this cradle of life is disappearing at an enormous rate. This is what the popular press has labeled as the "biodiversity" crisis.

Most of the debate centers on how fast a forest will recover after a major disturbance, such as logging, not on whether it will.

Some view the problem from only a utilitarian point of view. It is obvious that we depend on biodiversity for the most elementary aspects of existence—plants convert the sun's energy to a usable form, animals convert unusable plants to a product we can use, bacteria in our stomachs help digest our food. There are a host of other critical functions of life's diversity and furthermore, future utilitarian designs on biodiversity are most likely to follow the patterns of the past—medicines and genes for new crops being the obvious examples.

Yet even if these utilitarian concerns were absent, the spiritual concern that the world's biodiversity is being destroyed should be enough to drive us to action. Less than 50% of the original tropical rain forests of the world are left, and at the present rate of destruction almost all will be gone by 2025. Our families, our memories—indeed a piece of our humanness—will have been destroyed forever. For this reason many have sounded the alarm and called for action.

While we echo this same alarm, we are concerned that the calls for action may not be correctly placed. Indeed, many of these calls are based on one myth or another about what is causing rain forest destruction. We feel that these myths act to mask the true issue. In this viewpoint we present arguments against the five main myths of rain forest destruction and argue that a more complex understanding is necessary to grasp what is causing the destruction of the world's rain forests. So we begin with an analysis of the five myths and conclude with a description of "the causal web," the *true* cause of rain forest destruction.

Effects of logging

Myth One: Loggers and logging companies are decimating the rain forest.

Certainly the most immediate and visually spectacular cause of tropical rain forest destruction is logging. Cutting trees is nothing new. The use of rain forest wood has been traditional for most human societies in contact with these ecosystems. But the European invasion of tropical lands accelerated wood cutting enormously, as tropical woods began contributing to the development of the modern industrial society.[1]

The direct consequences of logging, apart from the obvious and dramatic visual effects, are largely unknown. Some facts are deducible from general ecological principles, and a handful of studies have actually measured a few of the consequences, but a detailed knowledge of the direct consequences of logging is lacking.

Laying the blame for the destruction of the forest on the peasant farmer is really blaming the victim.

What can be deduced from ecological principles is not that tropical forests are irreparably damaged by logging, but quite the contrary: tropical forests are potentially quite resilient to disturbance. While this is a debatable deduction, most of the debate centers on how fast a forest will recover after a major disturbance, such as logging, not on whether it will. The process of ecological succession inevitably begins after logging, and the proper question to ask, then, is: how long will it take for the forest to recover?

In analyzing the effects of logging, we cannot assume a uniform process. There are a variety of logging techniques, some likely to lead to rapid forest recovery, others necessitating a longer period for recovery. For example, local residents frequently chop down trees for their own use as fence posts, charcoal, or dugout canoes. Forest recovery after such an intrusion can be thought of as virtually instantaneous, since the removal of a single tree is similar to a tree dying of natural causes, a perfectly natural process that happens regularly in all forests. At the other extreme is clear cutting, the extraction of all trees in an area. Though the physical nature of a clear cut forest is spectacularly different from the mature forest, from other perspectives the damage is not quite as dramatic as it appears. The process of secondary succession that begins immediately after such logging leads rapidly to the establishment of secondary forest. A great deal of biological diversity is contained in a secondary forest. Indeed, a late secondary forest is likely to appear indistinguishable from an old-growth forest to all but the most sophisticated observer, even though it may have been initiated from a clear cut. Large expanses of secondary forest may even contain more biological diversity than similar expanses of old-growth forest.[2] No studies thus far have followed such an area to its return to a "mature" forest again,[3] but a reasonable estimate is that it would take something on the order of 40 to 80 years before the area begins to regain the structure of an old-growth forest.

Probably the most common type of commercial logging is not the clear cutting described above but, rather, selective logging. In an area of tropical forest that may contain 400 or more species of trees, only twenty or thirty will be of commercial importance.[4] Thus, a logging company usually seeks out areas with particularly large concentrations of the valuable species and ignores the rest. Often the wood is so valuable that it makes economic sense to build a road to extract just a few trees. Yet these roads offer new access to the forest for hunters, miners, and peasant agriculturists. In most situations this aspect of selective logging contributes most egregiously to deforestation, but it is obviously an *indirect* consequence of the logging operation itself.

A selectively logged forest is damaged, but not destroyed. Even a single year after the selective logging the forest begins taking on the appearance of a "real" forest. If no further cutting occurs, the selectively logged forest may regain the structural features of old growth after ten or twenty years. Although the scars of selective logging will remain for decades to a trained eye, the general structure of the forest may rapidly return. But this is not to say selective logging is, in the end, benign. The roads and partial clearings are obvious entrance points for peasant agriculture, as described below.

Peasant farmers

Myth Two: Peasant farmers are increasing in numbers and cut down rain forests to make farms to feed their families.

This myth is especially popular among neo-Malthusians [those who adhere to British economist Thomas Malthus's theory that population tends to grow much faster than the food supply]. The explosive growth in the population of poor people in most tropical countries of the world is seen as a consequence of the basic forces that cause populations to grow generally, and a simple extrapolation suggests that even if this is not the main problem now, it certainly will be if population growth is not somehow curtailed.

Debunking the neo-Malthusian myth is not our purpose here; that has been done well elsewhere.[5] Rather, laying the blame for the destruction of the forest on the peasant farmer is really blaming the victim. Peasant farmers in most rain forest areas are forced to farm under circumstances that are unfavorable, to say the least, from both an ecological and sociopolitical point of view.

At the outset, we must acknowledge the temptation to assume that, in rain forest areas, the potential for agriculture is great. Since there is neither winter nor lack of water, two of the main limiting factors for agriculture in other areas of the world, it is easy to conclude that production might very well be cornucopian. The tremendously lush vegetation of a tropical rain forest only heightens this impression, and indeed this perception may ultimately be valid. The ability to produce for twelve months of the year without worrying about irrigation is definitely a positive aspect to farming in such regions. But, so far at least, the woes are almost insurmountable, as most farmers forced to cultivate in rain forest areas can attest.

The first problem is the soils. Rain forest soils are usually acidic, made up of clay that cannot store nutrients well, and very low in organic matter.[6] Even if nutrients are added to the soil the will be utilized relatively inefficiently because of the acidity, and then they will be washed out of the system because of its low storage capacity.

This problem is actually exacerbated by the forest itself. Because tropical rain forest plants have grown in these poor soil conditions for millions of years, they have evolved mechanisms for storing the system's nutrients in their vegetative matter (leaves, stems, roots, etc.) If they did not, much of the nutrient material would simply wash out of the system and no longer be available to them. This means that a vast majority of the nutrients in the ecosystem are stored in plant material rather than in the soil.

Consequently when a forest is cut down and burned, the nutrients in the vegetation are immediately made available to any crops that have been planted. The crops grow vigorously at first, but any nutrients unused during the first growing season will tend to leach out of the system. The "poverty" of the soil only becomes evident during the second growing season. This pattern is especially invidious when migrant farmers from areas with relatively stable soils arrive in a rain forest area. The first year they may produce a bumper crop, which creates a false sense of security. Then, if the second year is not a complete failure, almost certainly the third or fourth is, and the farmer is forced to move on to cut down another piece of forest.

A second problem is insects, diseases and weeds. The magnitude of the pest problem is often not fully anticipated by farmers or planners, and it is only after problems arise that the surprised agronomists become concerned. This is unfortunate, since one of the few things we can predict with confidence is that when rain forest is converted to agriculture, many pests arrive. The herbivores that used to eat the plants of the rain forest are not eliminated when the forest is cut. They are representatives of the massive biodiversity of tropical rain forests, and the potential number of them is enormous. Herbivores can devastate farmers' fields, and are able to destroy an entire crop in days.

A third problem is that because of the uniformly moist and warm environment, organisms that cause crop diseases find rain forest habitats quite hospitable. Consequently, the potential for losing crops to disease is far greater than in more temperate climates. Finally, just as the hot, wet environment is agreeable for crops, it is also agreeable for competitive plants. Since no two plants can occupy the same space, frequently the crop falls victim to the more aggressive vines and grasses that colonize open areas in tropical rain forest zones. Weeds are thus an especially difficult problem.

About 90% of the current expansion [of Central American banana plantations] is into areas that had long ago been deforested.

These, then, are some of the ecological problems faced by the peasant farmer seeking to establish a farm in a rain forest area. Sociopolitical forces, however, are far more devastating. And most of those sociopolitical forces are associated with a different form of agriculture—modern export agriculture.

When a modern export agricultural operation is set up, it tends to do two things regarding labor. First, it purchases, or sometimes steals, land from local peasant farmers, thus forcing them to move onto more marginal lands, with the kinds of problems we described above. Second, it frequently requires more labor than is locally available, thus acting as a magnet to attract unemployed people from other regions. Indeed, in most rain forest areas this magnet effect is a far more important factor leading to increased local populations than population growth.

But the modern agricultural operation, as detailed in the following section, is subject to dramatic fluctuations in production, since it is usually intimately connected with world agricultural commodity markets. Thus, there is a highly variable need for this labor, which means that today's workers always face the prospect of becoming tomorrow's peasant farmers.

In the contemporary world most peasant farmers find themselves in this precarious position. While it is true that many indigenous groups have lived and farmed in rain forest areas for hundreds of years and certainly deserve the world's attention and support in their attempts at preserving traditional ways of life, the vast majority of poor peasant farmers today are not indigenous. Rather, they are people who have been marginalized by a politico-economic system that needs them to serve as laborers when times are good, and to take care of themselves when times are not. As long as times are good, the banana workers of Central America have jobs. But when economies sour, many of those banana workers suddenly become peasant farmers.

So in the end, the myth of the peasant farmers causing rain forest destruction is perhaps true in the narrow sense that a knitting needle causes yarn to form a sweater. But little understanding of what really drives the process is gained from the simple observation that a peasant's ax can chop a rain forest tree.

Export agriculture

Myth Three: The transformation of rain forests into large-scale export agriculture is the main factor leading to deforestation.

Given the above description of how peasant agriculture is driven by industrialized agricultural activities, it is no wonder that many have concluded that the modern export agricultural system is the ultimate culprit. Furthermore, the images of large cattle ranchers purposefully burning Amazon rain forests to make cattle pastures fuels this interpretation. Again, there is some merit to this position. However, we feel that it, too, is an inappropriate window through which to view the problem of rain forest destruction.

The direct action of large modern agricultural enterprises is not really as involved in direct rain forest destruction as is popularly believed. Burning Amazon rain forests to replace them with cattle ranches is certainly an example of the direct destruction of rain forests by "big" agriculture. But the vast majority of modern agricultural transformations in tropical areas are confined to areas that had already been converted to agriculture. Developers of expanding banana plantations of Central America claim, for example, to be cutting no primary forest at all. While we doubt their full sincerity, it does seem that about 90% of the current expansion is into areas that had long ago been deforested. Attributing direct deforestation to them is, as they argue, probably quite unfair. On the other hand, their activities are not totally unrelated to the problem, as can be easily seen from a closer examination of their underlying structure.

The basic structure of modern agriculture is frequently misunderstood because of an overly romantic notion of agriculture—the small, independent, family farm, rich with tradition and a work ethic that even a Puritan could be impressed with. Such romanticism is fueled by a confusion between farming and agriculture.

Farming is a resource transformation process in which land, seed, and labor are converted into, for example, peanuts. It is Farmer Brown cultivating the land, sowing the seed, and harvesting the peanuts. Agriculture is the decision to invest money in this year's peanut production; the use of a tractor and cultivator to prepare the land; an automatic seeder for planting; application of herbicides, insecticides, fungicides, nematodes and bactericides to kill unwanted pieces of the ecology; automatic harvest of the commodity; sale of the commodity to a processing company where it is ground up and emulsifiers, taste enhances, stabilizers and preservatives are added; packing in convenient "pleasing-to-the-consumer" jars; and, finally, marketing under a sexy brand name. In short, while farming is the production of peanuts from the land, agriculture is the production of peanut butter from petroleum.[7] Over the last two hundred years, and especially in the last fifty, much farming has been transformed into agriculture.

It is difficult to lay the full blame on local governments.

The consequence of this evolution is that modern agriculture is remarkably intrusive on local ecologies. Take, for example, the establishment of a banana plantation. When the banana export business began, local peasant farmers grew most of the bananas and sold them to shipping companies. Gradually, the shipping companies turned into the banana producers, with huge areas devoted to the monocultural production of this single crop. To establish a modern banana plantation it is often necessary to construct a complex system of hydrological control wherein the soil is leveled and crisscrossed with drainage channels, significantly altering the physical nature of the soil. Contemporary banana production even includes burying plastic tubing in the ground to eliminate the natural variability in subsurface water depth. Metal monorails hang from braces placed into cement footings to haul the bunches of bananas. To avert fungal diseases, heavy use of fungicides is required, and because of the large scale of the operation chemical methods of pest control are the preferred option. The banana plants create an almost complete shade cover and thus replace all residual vegetation. Pesticide application is sometimes intense, other times almost absent, depending on conditions, but over the long run one can expect an enormous cumulative input of pesticides, the long-term consequences of which are unknown but likely to be unhealthy for both workers and the environment.

A major social transformation is also required. Banana production tends to promote a local "overpopulation crisis" by encouraging a great deal of migration into the area. As the international market for bananas ebbs and flows, workers are alternatively hired and fired. When fired, there is little alternative economic opportunity in banana zones, and displaced workers must either look for a piece of land to farm, or migrate to the cities to join the swelling ranks of shanty town dwellers.

Thus, the direct effect of most modern agricultural activities is not inexorably linked with the cutting and burning of rain forests, despite some obvious and spectacular examples of where it indeed is. More importantly, the overall operation of the modern agricultural system is integrated into a bigger picture. It is that bigger picture that we must examine to understand the causes of rain forest destruction, as we argue in the final section of this viewpoint.

Local governments

Myth Four: Local governments institute policies that cause rain forests to be destroyed.

Probably the most cited example of local government policy that promotes deforestation is that of the infamous transmigration programs of the Indonesian government, in which hundreds of thousands of Javanese farmers have been displaced to the exceedingly poor soils of Kalimantan.[8] However, most local government programs in forestry and agriculture are frequently dictated by very specific economic and political forces that are effectively beyond the control of local governments. Once those forces are understood, it is difficult to lay the full blame on local governments. They may be corrupt, they may be inefficient, but in fact their hands are frequently tied by forces beyond their control.

Given today's global interconnectedness, in order to understand the Third World we must view it as embedded in the modern industrial system. In that system the people who provide the labor in the production processes are not the same people who provide the tools, machines and factories. The former are the workers in the factories, the latter are the owners of the factories. The owners of the machines and tools directly make the management decisions about all production processes. A good manager tries to minimize all production costs, including the cost of labor.

However, the owners of the factories face a complicated and contradictory task. While factory workers constitute a cost of production to be minimized, they also participate, along with the multitudes of other workers in society, in the consumption of products. In trying to maximize profits, factory owners are concerned that their factories' products sell for a high price. This can only happen if workers, in general, are making a lot of money. In contrast to what is desired at the level of the factory, the opposite goal is sought at the level of society. Factory owners must wear two hats, then: one as owners of the factories, and another as members of a social class. Owners wish the laborers to receive as little as possible, but members of the social class benefit if laborers in general receive as much as possible (to enable them to purchase the products produced in the factory). This has long been recognized as one of the classic contradictions of a modern economy.

The situation in much of the Third World appears superficially similar. For the most part we are dealing with agrarian economies in which there are two obvious social classes, those who produce crops for export like cotton, coffee, tea, rubber, bananas, chocolate, beef, and sugar, and those who produce food for their own consumption on their own small farms and, when necessary, provide the labor for export crop producers.

The typical arrangement in the Developed World is an articulated economy, while that in the Third World is disarticulated, in that the two main sectors of the economy are not articulated or connected with one another. The banana company does not really care whether its workers make enough money to buy bananas; that is not its market. The banana company cares that the workers of the Developed World have purchasing power, because those are the people expected to buy most of the bananas.

This disarticulation, or dualism, helps to explain the differences between analogous classes in the First and Third Worlds. Flower producers in Colombia do not concern themselves much over the fact that their workers cannot buy their products. On the other hand, the factory owners in the U.S., whether they be private factories or government owned and/or subsidized industries, care quite a lot that the working class has purchasing power. General Motors "cares" that the general population in the U.S. can afford to buy cars. Naturally they aim to pay their own workers as little as possible, but that goal is balanced by their wish for the workers in general to be good consumers.

Seeing this structure at the national level in an underdeveloped country causes one to realize that one of the main, sometimes only, sources of capital to create a civil society is from agricultural exports. Because of the disarticulated nature of the economy the dream of development based on internally derived consumer demand is pie in the sky, and any realist must acknowledge that the only conceivable source of capital to invest in growth must come from exports. And most frequently agricultural exports are the only possibility.

Herein derives the need for Third World governments to continue expanding this export agriculture. This need is an inevitable consequence of the underlying structure of the general world system. Thus to blame local governments for initiating policies that are ultimately damaging to rain forests may be technically correct in that those policies frequently do just what the critics say they do—destroy rain forests. But taking a larger view we see that local governments are effectively constrained to do exactly that. Indeed, we predict that most of today's critics would wind up promoting the very same programs the local governments are currently promoting, if they were suddenly pushed into the same position the local governments currently find themselves.

International agencies

Myth Five: Decisions made by international agencies cause rain forest destruction.

As before, there is some truth to this position. As well documented, although not yet "retrospected" by [former World Bank president] Mr. Robert F. McNamara, the World Bank has left a trail of rain forest destruction in the wake of its many socially and economically destructive programs in the Third World.[9] From the point of view of the decision making agencies, they, along with other agencies involved in the overall problem, seem to be boxed in by circumstances.

The climate for investment is variable in the Developed World. There are times when it is difficult to find profitable investments at home. At such times it is useful to have alternatives to investment. The Third World is one source for those opportunities. The Developed World, because of its basic structure, tends to go through cycles of bust and boom, sometimes severe, other times merely annoying. During low economic times, where is an investor supposed to invest? The Third World provides a sink for investments during rough times in the First World. This is why the dualism of the Third World is a "functional dualism." It functions to provide an escape valve for investors from the Developed World. The West German entrepreneur who started an ornamental plant farm in Costa Rica, on which former peasant farmers work as night watchmen, invested his money in the Third World because opportunities in his native Germany were scarce at the time. What would he have done had there been no peasants willing to work for practically nothing, and no Costa Rica willing to accept his investments at very low taxation? Clearly Costa Rica is, for him, a place to make his capital work until the situation clears up in Germany. Union Carbide located its plant in Bhopal, India, and not in Grand Rapids, Michigan. U.S. pesticide companies export to Third World countries insecticides that have been banned at home. U.S. pharmaceutical companies pollute the ground water in Puerto Rico because they cannot do so (at least not so easily) in the United States. In all cases, Third World people are forced to accept such arrangements, largely because of their extremely underdeveloped economy.

The World Bank has left a trail of rain forest destruction.

With this analysis, the origin of the Third World as an outgrowth of European expansion (while a correct and useful historical point of view), can be seen as not the only factor to be considered. Even today, the maintenance of the Third World is a consequence of the way our world system operates. The Developed World remains successful at economic development for two reasons. First, because it has an articulated economy, and second, because it is able to weather the storm of economic crisis by seeking investment opportunities in the Third World. The Third World, in contrast, has been so unsuccessful because its economy is disarticulated, lacking the connections that would make it grow in the same way as the Developed World. Yet at a more macro scale, the dualism of the Third World is quite functional, in that it maintains the opportunity for investors from the Developed World to use the Third World as an escape valve in times of crisis. Indeed, it appears that the Developed World remains developed, at least in part, specifically because the Underdeveloped World is underdeveloped.

Given this structure, what really can be expected of international agencies? Their goal is usually stated in very humanitarian rhetoric. But their more basic goal has to be the preservation of the system that gives them their station in life. That is, above and beyond the stated goals of the World Bank or the IMF [International Monetary Fund] or the FAO [Food and Agriculture Organization], there must be a commitment to keep the world organized in its current state. Their activities can thus be viewed as trying to solve problems within the context of the current system. They thus become part of what preserves that system.

We should not expect large international agencies to be promoting such causes as land reform for peasant agriculture or labor standard regulations for export agriculture. Indeed, such proposals would be at odds with the manner in which the current world system is functioning, and would represent a legitimate challenge to the existence of the agency itself. Viewed from this perspective, the international agencies are just as boxed in as the local governments. The world system is functioning as well today as it was at the end of World War II—according to the standards adopted by those who benefit from its current structure.

The web of causality

In reading our demythologization of the above five myths, the reader has undoubtedly noted that there really is something valid about each of the myths. Loggers do cut trees down, peasant agriculturists do clear and burn forests, export agriculturists do cut down primary rain forests, local governments do encourage export agriculture, and international agencies do promote programs that destroy rain forests. But our attempt was not to disprove these myths per se, but rather to disprove the idea that any one of them could be the ultimate cause of rain forest destruction. Indeed, in each case we have emphasized not the direct consequences of the agency involved but, rather, the indirect connections that tie each of the agencies into a web of interaction.

We agree with I. Wallerstein's[10] general assessment that the world is intricately connected, that it no longer makes sense to try understanding isolated pockets, such as nations, and, we add, that isolated thematic pockets are similarly incomprehensible unless embedded in this global framework. For this reason, attempts at understanding tropical rain forest destruction in isolation have largely failed. As should be clear by now, the fate of the rain forest is intimately tied to various agricultural activities, which are embedded in larger structures, some retaining a connection to agriculture, some not. Our position is that there is multiple causation of rain forest destruction, with logging, peasant agriculture, export agriculture, domestic sociopolitical forces, international socio-economic relations, and other factors intricately connected with one another in a "web of causality." This web is key to understanding why we face the problem of rain forest destruction in the first place.

Political action must focus on the web of causality and eschew single issue foci.

The most elementary features of that web are illustrated in figure 1. At the bottom of the figure we see that damaged rain forests will recuperate if not further damaged, but recuperate far more slowly if further modified by agriculture. The damaged rain forests themselves are created by either logging or modern agriculture and further cleared by peasant farmers. But the latter's activities are a consequence of the opportunities created by logging as well as the ups and downs of the international market that cause the hiring and firing of workers. Modern agriculture needs those workers, as well as the land that it buys or steals from peasant farmers. Viewed as a web of causality, it is quite pointless to try to identify a single entity as the "true" cause of rain forest destruction. The true cause is the web itself.

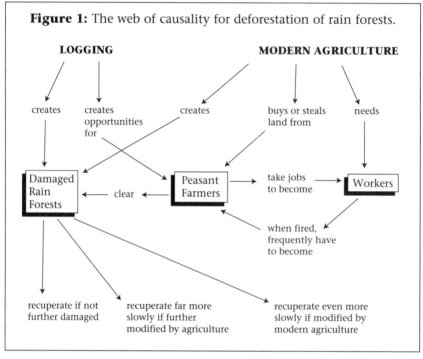

Figure 1: The web of causality for deforestation of rain forests.

Yet even this is an oversimplified picture. The web of causality is far larger and more complex. The farmers, loggers, modern agriculture and workers of figure 1 represent just a subweb. The subweb is ultimately embedded in a larger web that includes the international banking system, national governments, the U.S. and other Developed World governments, as well as consumers and investors in the Developed World. This is the true web of causality, and it is complicated and interconnected. Tweaking one strand is not likely to bring the whole structure down. Fighting a concerted battle to restructure the entire nature of the web is the only alternative.

Furthermore, seeing the entire web of causality enables those engaged in highly focused political action to see their actions in relation to other actions, perhaps evoking an analysis of consequences that may be dramatic, even though quite indirect. For example, organizing consumer boycotts can be seen as clearly attacking the connection between consumers and modern export agriculture. But following through the logic of the web also suggests that a successful consumer boycott may likewise reduce the need of modern agriculture for workers, thus creating more peasant farmers, who will likely clear more forest. If a careful analysis of this situation reveals that the loss of jobs will be severe, the political action agenda might then be expanded to form alliances with a local farm

worker union calling for job security or a political movement seeking secure land ownership for the increased number of peasant farmers that
will surely be created if the boycott is a success.

The political action plan

This analysis is meaningless without a program of political action. Political action must focus on the web of causality and eschew single issue foci.
Calls for boycotts of tropical timbers or bananas need to be coupled with
actions to change investment patterns and international banking pressures. Above all, political action plans must be formulated so they do not
make the situation worse—certainly a conceivable, perhaps even likely,
consequence of any action, given the complex nature of the web of
causality. It appears obvious that political action needs to be focused not
only on rain forests and the subjects traditionally associated with them,
but also on social justice. The same peasant farmers who formed the back-
bone of the Vietnamese liberation forces or the Salvadoran guerrillas are
the ones who are forced into the marginal existence that compels them
to continually move into the forests. So the same issues that compelled
progressive organizers in the past to form solidarity committees and anti-
war protests are the issues that must be addressed if the destruction of
rain forests is to be stopped.

Just as the most effective political action in the past was organized in
conjunction with and to some extent under the leadership of the people
for whom social justice was being sought, so today political action should
be coordinated with those same people. As that coordination proceeds, the
alliances that grow will inevitably lead to the reformulation of goals,
which the rain forest conservation activist must acknowledge and respect.
Local people, quite obviously, must recognize something about the rain
forest that is in their best interest to preserve, and it is the job of the progressive organizer to construct the political action so that such value is evident. In short, the alliance between the people who live in and around the
rain forest and those from the outside who seek to stop the tide of rain forest destruction must be a two way alliance. If the people who live around
the Lacandon forest in Mexico, for example, have as their major goal the
reformulation of the Mexican political system, the rain forest conservationist must join the political movement to change that system—something that many would see as distant from the original goal of preserving
rain forests. Political action to preserve rain forests, under the framework
of the web of causality, will inevitably involve the serious preservationist
in social justice issues, many of which initially may have seemed only mar-
ginally associated with the problem of rain forest destruction. Recalling the
old slogan, "If you want peace, work for justice," we hope someday to hear,
for example, "Save Mexican rain forests, support the Zapatistas," or "If you
want to save Cuba's rain forests, break the illegal U.S. blockade."

Notes

1. Westoby, 1989.

2. Some ecologists think that the actual number of species in an ecosystem
   increases as ecological succession proceeds, but only to a point. After that

critical point, the diversity actually decreases, leading to the conclusion that a very old forest may be less diverse than a younger one.

3. There is a problem with the definition here. Most ecologists today eschew the notion of a "mature" forest, and simply speak of "old growth." The notion of maturity implies something about a directed developmental sequence that does not fit well with what we now know about tropical rain forest succession.

4. There are exceptions to this rule. Many swampy forests are characterized by the presence of only a few species. The biggest exception are the Southeast Asian Dipterocarp forests, where the vast majority of trees in the forest belong to a single plant family, characterized by very large and straight trunks, a logger's delight.

5. Rosset, 1994; Murdoch, 1980; Lappé, F.M. and J. Collins, 1977; Lappé, F.M. and R. Schurman, 1988.

6. There is some debate about the question of organic matter in rain forest soils. The rate of decomposition of organic matter is about twice the rate it is in a normal temperate zone situation, and thus it is only natural to expect the standing crop of organic matter to be less in the rain forest. Some authors have questioned this basic assumption (e.g. National Research Council, 1993). On the other hand, all are in agreement that once the forest is cleared for agriculture, whatever organic matter was actually there rapidly disappears from the soil.

7. This is the imagery first provided by Lewontin, 1982.

8. Kiddell-Monroe and Kiddell-Monroe, 1993.

9. Rich, 1994.

10. Wallerstein, 1980.

References

Kiddell-Monroe, S. and R. Kiddell-Monroe. 1993. "Indonesia: Land Rights and Development." in Colchester, M. and L. Lohmann (eds.) *The Struggle for Land and the Fate of the Forests*. World Rainforest Movement and Zed Books, London.

Lappé, F.M. and J. Collins. 1977. *Food First: Beyond the Myth of Scarcity*. Houghton Mifflin, Boston.

Lappé, F.M. and R. Shurman. 1988. *Taking Population Seriously*. Institute for Food and Development Policy, San Francisco.

Lewontin, R. 1982. "Agricultural Research and the Penetration of Capital." *Science for the People* 14:12–17.

Murdoch, W. 1980. *Poverty of Nations: Population, Hunger, and Development*. Johns Hopkins Univ. Press, Baltimore.

National Research Council. 1993. *Sustainable Agriculture and the Environment in the Humid Tropics*. National Academy Press, Washington, D.C.

Rich, B. 1994. *Mortgaging the Earth: The World Bank, Environmental Impoverishment, and the Crisis of Development*. Beacon Press, Boston.

Rosset, P. et al. 1994. "Myths and Root Causes: Hunger, Population and Development." Institute for Food and Development Policy, Oakland.

Wallerstein, I. 1980. *The Modern World System II: Mercantilism and the Consolidation of the European World-Economy*, 1260–1750. Academic Press, New York.

Westoby, J. 1989. *Introduction to World Forestry*. Basil Blackwell Ltd., Oxford.

2

Asian Logging Companies Are Cutting Rainforests Worldwide

Timothy M. Ito and Margaret Loftus

Timothy M. Ito and Margaret Loftus are reporters for U.S. News & World Report *weekly magazine.*

Logging companies from Indonesia, Malaysia, and other Asian countries are being granted generous concessions to cut rainforests in Africa, Central America, South America, and the South Pacific. These companies frequently ignore principles of sustainable forestry aimed at minimizing environmental damage. Some logging companies flout regulations, evade taxation, and offer bribes in order to cut more forests and increase profits.

It wasn't until the Maya villagers in San Jose, Belize, saw the bulldozers tearing through the jungle that they discovered the government had granted a logging concession on their ancestral lands. Within months, says Juan Sam, he was seeing three daily truckloads of logs pulling out of the once dense rain forest near the village of Santa Anna where he'd hunted and fished all his life.

Facing dwindling timber stocks and tighter environmental regulations in overcut forests at home, an army of Asian timber companies is plunging into the world's remaining rain forests. Leading the charge overseas are Malaysian and Indonesian multinationals, some with less than stellar environmental records. Juan Sam's new neighbors were loggers from a Malaysian firm, Atlantic Industries; other Asian firms are aggressively targeting other spots in Central America, the Congo Basin, and the South Pacific.

Extensive operations

What sets these multinationals apart from others that have staged forays into the rain forests in the past is the sheer scale of their operations. In

Papua New Guinea, Malaysia's largest logger, Rimbunan Hijau, now controls at least 60 percent of the government's 21.5 million-acre forestry concession area through more than 20 subsidiaries. In Guyana, the Barama Co. (a joint venture between Malaysian logging giant Samling Strategic Corp. and Korean trading company Sunkyong Ltd.) cuts on a concession slightly larger than the state of Connecticut, about 4.2 million acres. All told, Asian firms have already snapped up an estimated 30 million acres (of the 1.38 billion-acre total) in the Amazon Basin.

Neglecting the basics

The problem, say forestry experts, isn't that logging in tropical forests is inherently bad. But these firms are given such leeway that they often neglect the most elementary principles of sustainable forestry. Basics like mapping trees to be cut, building roads with as little disruption to the forest as possible, and felling trees into gaps in the canopy are routinely ignored by the Asian firms, say foresters who have studied their practices. "None of them are doing what they should," says Nigel Sizer of the World Resources Institute in Washington, D.C.

In Belize, the local Audubon Society claimed that Atlantic Industries was illegally cutting down protected sapodillas—the "chicle" trees once harvested heavily for their sap, a substitute for rubber and later the main ingredient in chewing gum. The group also charged the loggers had cut within a 20-meter restricted zone along streams, which can cause massive erosion of banks. Atlantic Industries denies felling any protected trees, but a 2-mile hike into its timber-felling operation near Santa Anna reveals stacks of logs, including sapodillas, piled next to bulldozed tracks. The logs, some 200 years old, were left to rot last season by loggers in their hasty retreat at the onset of the rains.

These firms are given such leeway that they often neglect the most elementary principles of sustainable forestry.

Just one season's felling has taken a toll. The jungle here was once lush and shady, says one Maya leader, Julian Cho; villagers had to use machetes to clear a path through underbrush and saw grass. Today, bulldozed tracks of red clay guide visitors into a sunnier and sparser place—evidence that here the Malaysians have almost free rein. Hunting, a way of life for the Mayas who inhabit nearby villages, has become more difficult because the noise of the machinery forces wildlife deeper into the bush. And villagers from Canejo, about 10 miles downstream, were without drinking water in 1996 when logging operations near streams filled the headwaters of the Temash River with mud.

Logging violations are frequent, local villagers say, not only because there are so few government monitors but also because some firms disguise the size of the lands they actually control. Maya villagers and other concession holders say that Atlantic Industries, for example, logs and controls several areas outside of its own 24,000-acre lease, including a

159,000-acre neighboring concession and at least two other large plots of land that total 30,000 acres. And unlike its own concession—which does have a nominal forestry-management plan—none of these other plots are even subject to government guidelines for cutting.

Sweetheart deals

Asian loggers are hardly unique in disregarding sound environmental practices. But they have been particularly aggressive in moving into some of the world's poorest countries with the most lax enforcement of environmental regulations—and in cutting cozy deals with the government agencies that hand out logging concessions. Many of the agreements between countries like Belize and firms like Atlantic Industries are consummated in private—and, at least in Atlantic Industries' case, over the objections of local experts who reviewed the proposed contracts. In 1995, the company approached Belize's forestry department with a proposal to log in the uncut rain forest of the country's southern Toledo district. A February 1995 report by the government's technical forestry consultant was highly critical: "It clearly lacks professional preparation and analysis," wrote Neil Bird, the consultant. "It is not something one would expect from an investor who is preparing to invest $3.5 million [$1.8 million U.S.] in a timber operation. . . . I have serious doubts about the credibility of this company."

Yet despite that unfavorable recommendation—and warnings from the forestry department—the transaction was pushed through in April 1995.

Atlantic's manager in Belize, Wong Sing Ling, admits that his company operations, which also include a huge local sawmill, cannot be profitable logging in just the restricted reserve area but says his firm's actions have been entirely proper. Taking a break from an employee volleyball game at the company mill one drizzly afternoon, the mild-mannered Malaysian says that Belize reminds him a lot of home. He says he can't understand what the uproar is all about, his voice rising above the din of bulldozers in the background. However, Wong would not address questions about the relationship of Atlantic Industries with other license holders in the Toledo district.

Bribes are simply a way of life for the logging companies.

In other parts of the world, Asian logging companies have drawn fierce criticism for their sharp business practices. In July 1994, for example, Tony C.T. Yeong, an executive from a Malaysian multinational, the Berjaya Group, was expelled from the Solomon Islands for allegedly attempting to bribe the country's minister of commerce. Press accounts at the time reported that Yeong—who claimed the money was a gift—had offered the official about $3,000 to help further the company's takeover plans of a local logging company. When contacted about the matter, Berjaya officials insisted that it "never gave [Yeong] any authority to negotiate deals in this manner." Yeong has since resigned, and Berjaya pulled out of the Solomons.

Guyana's commissioner of forests, Clayton Hall, says bribes are simply a way of life for the logging companies. "They come in and believe they can pay off Third World officials," says Hall, who oversees the Barama concession and two other major Asian timber company leases. He says that he is offered a bribe nearly every day he is on the job. Of course, Hall says, he never accepts it.

Some of the Asian companies have also been adept at shell games that have allowed them to evade local scrutiny and taxation. In 1992, 20 Malaysian timber companies were forced to pay large back taxes in their own country on income they had previously stashed away in shell companies in loosely regulated places like the British Virgin Islands or Hong Kong.

Nobody loves a logger

The companies and their supporters complain that they are simply easy targets for criticism. "Anybody who attains any sort of high profile immediately becomes the whipping boy of environmentalists. And these Asian companies are now the whipping boys," says Robert Waffle, staff vice president of government and environmental affairs at the International Wood Products Association. Wong Kieyik, a manager at WTK Group, says his company, which applied for a 741,000-acre timber concession in Brazil, has already come under fire from environmental groups, though "we haven't even cut down a single leaf yet." The Barama Co. says it is sensitive to environmental concerns and has even hired an environmental group, the Edinburgh Center for Tropical Forests, to monitor its forestry-management practices.

Back in Belize, the roar of the bulldozers and the whir of the chainsaws continue unabated. Local forestry experts say that the irresponsible cutting practices are already doing irreparable harm to the rain forest. In 20 years, predicts soil scientist Charles Wright, there could be a regrowth of secondary trees—maybe even a canopy—but the richness of the forest will be lost. Ironically, Asian firms like Atlantic Industries may be unnecessarily doing away with the very resource that sustains them. Company officials insist they are logging in Belize for the long run. But if there is little left to log, the only choice Atlantic Industries may have is to move on—move on, perhaps, to the next poor, developing country.

3
Mahogany Logging Threatens the Amazon Rainforests and Tribes

George Marshall

George Marshall is the international campaign coordinator for the Rainforest Foundation in New York City.

The logging of mahogany trees is a major cause of deforestation in Brazil's Amazon rainforests. As mature mahogany trees are cut, little seed is left for the regeneration of forests. In their quest for mahogany, logging companies are breaking laws and taking advantage of Indians. Mahogany logging harms Amazon tribes through the spread of disease, social disintegration, and violence against Indians.

There is a very strong case to be made against Brazilian mahogany. Logging for mahogany is rapidly becoming the most significant cause of deforestation in the Brazilian Amazon, both because of the direct effects of logging on the forest and because the access logging roads provide for further clearing. Mahogany cutters are working in breach of all aspects of Brazilian law, and wherever they have entered the forests they have brought violence and disease to the local Indian populations, including some of the most remote and vulnerable people in the world.

In most of the Amazon, logging would not be economically viable were it not for the high price of mahogany. If the markets for mahogany disappeared, there is every reason to believe that most of these areas and their peoples would remain undisturbed.

The key consideration for British people is that it is largely the very high demand for mahogany in Britain that is fueling this market. There is little demand for mahogany in Brazil, and, of the 80% that is exported, 56% is consumed by Britain.

It is only rarely that the consumers of just one country play such a decisive role in the destruction of the environment of another. It is even rarer for the demand in one country for just one product to have such a

From George Marshall, "The Case Against Mahogany," June 1994, at http://www.chu.cam.ac.uk/ home/hgd20/case.html, June 11, 1997. Reprinted by permission of the author.

decisive role. Many people in Britain are horrified when consumers in other countries have such an effect; for example the Japanese taste for whale meat, and the demand for endangered animals for Asian aphrodisiacs. Yet, in respect to mahogany, Britain is no different. Because of a traditional demand for a luxury product, Britain is playing a major role in the destruction of the world's largest and most precious rainforest, and the immeasurable richness of its life.

There can be no doubt that a successful British campaign on just this one timber species could measurably reduce rainforest destruction. This situation is virtually unique in the rainforest campaign.

Mahogany species

The two main South American mahogany species are Swietenia macrophylla and Swietenia mahogani. They have been traded as mahogany for over four centuries and are possibly the most valuable South American timber species. The initial trade up until the 19th century was in S. mahogani, especially under the commercial names of Cuban and Honduran mahogany. S. mahogani has suffered a reduction in the numbers and quality of its remaining stands over its entire range. Due to the continual removal of the best specimens, it is now largely a much-branched "bushy" tree unsuitable for timber production and considered as a weed (Styles 1981).

With the steady decline in both the quality and quantity of S. mahogani, S. macrophylla has become the main species sold as South American mahogany in Britain, and is rapidly following the same course.

The natural distribution of Swietenia macrophylla is in a band across the southern Amazon—from close to Brazil's east coast to the Bolivian border—through the far western Amazon, then narrowing through Ecuador and Colombia to central Venezuela, crossing the Darien Peninsula and occurring on the eastern seaboard of Central America (Lamb 1966).

Commercial pressures have degraded most indigenous stands of S. macrophylla throughout its range. In Capobianco, Venezuela, its population has declined by ⅔ in less than 15 years, and may be gone by the year 2000, though it is still abundant in the high western plains. In Peru, there has been a drastic fall in populations and it has become rare in Colombia, Costa Rica and Guatemala due to overexploitation, much of it illegal. Little is known of its current population in Mexico, though it is likely to have declined in proportion to Mexico's tropical forests, which now cover only 20% of their former area. Only in Brazil and Bolivia are there still large populations, but here too logging is rapidly reducing its range (Campbell 1992).

As a result, S. macrophylla has been listed by the International Board for Plant Genetic Resources (IBPGR) as a high priority species for genetic resource conservation. Brazil listed it as a vulnerable species in the Annex of the Convention on Nature Protection and Wildlife Preservation in the Western Hemisphere.

The main attempt to restrict the exploitation of the species was the 1992 proposal of the USA and Costa Rica to list all Swietenia species in Appendix II of the Convention on International Trade in Endangered Species (CITES), which would ensure the close monitoring of its trade.

This move is a preliminary to its listing on Appendix I, which would ban all trade. Despite having the support of the EC [European Community] and Brazil, the proposal failed because of intensive lobbying by American timber importers and the Bolivian government. However, many exporting nations have already placed restrictions on the trade of Swietenia spp [species], especially as unprocessed logs.

Although mahogany has a wide natural range of over 80,000 km^2, the range in which its harvest is commercially viable is far smaller. Government officials claim that mahogany is close to commercial exploitation in the accessible areas in which it is legally exploitable, which has led to very widespread illegal logging in Indian reserves (Monbiot 1992).

Highly destructive logging

According to observers and researchers, logging for tropical hardwoods is becoming the most significant cause of deforestation in the Brazilian Amazon (Padua, Anderson 1992).

In the past, the timber industry has played a relatively minor role in Amazonian deforestation, especially compared with cattle ranching, regional grand plan "development" programs, and large scale dam and mining projects. There are some indications that overall deforestation in the Brazilian Amazon may be slowing. The Brazilian government has reserved most of the tax breaks for cattle ranching and has an ambitious program for the demarcation of tribal lands. Agencies now show greater caution in funding large scale development projects in the area, though such projects still continue. Yet, the battle to save the Amazon is far from over. Mahogany cutting is now rapidly taking over the role of opening intact forest areas, providing access for settlers, and has become an important factor in the economies of further expansion of ranching.

Logging for mahogany is basically a "grab it and run operation" with highly destructive felling practices. A study in the south of Para found that for each mahogany tree removed, 28 other trees were seriously damaged, most of them toppled or uprooted. One thousand four hundred fifty square meters of forest were affected by the cutting of every mahogany tree (Verissimo 1992). As most mature mahogany trees are removed by the cutters, and logging takes place before the tree's fruiting season, little seed is left for regeneration. S. macrophylla seedlings have a high mortality, and, throughout its range, logging has led to a considerable fall in the population. Verissimo et al. conclude that "considering natural mortality, it is unlikely that this stock could produce a second harvest" (Verissimo 1992). Such destructive logging methods are nearly universal in the tropics, but in this case it is unlikely that there would be any logging at all in much of the forest in which mahogany grows were it not for the mahogany extraction (Verissimo 1992, Albrechtsen 1991).

Logging is now the principal means by which new agricultural frontiers are being established in Amazonia: colonists and ranchers make use of the roads cut through previously inaccessible regions, and clear the forest the loggers have opened (Plowden, Kusada 1989; Uhl 1990; Verissimo 1992). Because mahogany is widely distributed at low densities, logging requires excessive road access, with up to 400 km between forest and mills (Uhl 1990). In the case of logging in the Xingu area, 130.5 km of primary roads and 173 km of secondary roads were opened for the extraction of 5999 magno (mahogany) trees (Vidal, Giannini 1992).

There are eyewitness accounts of colonists following these logging roads. Fifteen hundred families followed Bannach into the River Iriri area of Arara territory and settled along its 90 km logging access road. Bannach's road was built in conjunction with the Rondonian colonisation program (Monbiot 1992). In Paragominas, the profits from mahogany logging are helping to subsidise and expand uneconomic cattle ranching (Uhl 1990).

In a number of cases the cutters have actively encouraged colonists to follow them to provide cheap labour and protection from the Indians and authorities. Claiming that they are just a small part of the wider invasion, the cutters shelter behind the political difficulties involved in the removal of colonists from reserves (Monbiot 1992). In the Alto Turiacu Reserve, in Para state, the timber cutters were followed by 1,100 colonists and ranchers (*Mensageiro* No. 67, January/February 1991). In the Guapore Reserve in Rondonia, 50 families of colonists moved up the logging roads at the instigation of the loggers, and 400 speculators staked claims to the land in the reserve, erecting signs along the roads (Rasmusson 1989a).

Officials from the Brazilian Department for Indigenous Affairs (FUNAI) claim that there is little hope of preventing the disintegration of indigenous societies in the southern Amazon while the mahogany trade continues unchecked (Sydney Possuelo, President of FUNAI, pers. comm., FUNAI Belem and FUNAI Altimira, pers. comm., cited Monbiot 1992).

Disease, social disintegration, and violence

Almost the entire adult population of the Surui people of the Sete de Setembro Reserve has contracted one or another venereal disease, and 20% of the population is suffering from tuberculosis (*Porantim*, September 1991). The population of the Surui has fallen by 90% in the 20 years since first contact, but the recent outbreaks have been blamed by the Indians themselves on the presence of loggers in their lands.

The Uru Eu Wau Wau are believed to have lost half their numbers since first contact in 1981, from diseases introduced by both timber cutters and colonists (Survival International 1991).

There have been epidemics of tuberculosis and leishmaniasis reported among the Marubo in the Javari Valley and widespread measles and flu complicated by bronchial pneumonia among the Matis (*Mensageiro* No. 68, March/April 1991).

The easternmost Arara are suffering severely from serious flu outbreaks following contacts between them and employees of the several logging firms invading their lands (*O Liberal* 10.11.88).

In 1991, 12 of the 188 Kulina of the River Jurua in Amazonas state died of whooping cough and malaria introduced by the invaders associated with the mahogany industry (*Porantim*, September 1991).

Twenty percent of the Hahaitesu-Nambiquara in Rondonia have died since 1987 through diseases introduced by timber cutters and colonists (CEDI 1992).

In most reserves in which Indians are regularly dealing with cutters, alcoholism is a problem, as white rum is handed out or traded for mahogany (CEDI 1992; *Porantim,* November 1991; *Aconteceu Especial* 18).

Having used the forest to meet all their needs, Indians can become dependent on a cash economy without cash, and many are tempted to sell other rights to their lands—such as mining concessions—in order to keep themselves alive. Young Indians come to lose respect for their own culture. They "are dazzled by the political power the timber cutter gives them. For them the timber cutter is the overall chief" (Vidal, Giannini 1992).

Logging for mahogany is basically a "grab it and run operation" with highly destructive felling practices.

There have been a large number of cases of Indians being murdered by timber cutters. In some of these cases there has been violence on both sides and mutual vendettas.

• In the Javari Park, Amazonas, in 1986, one Indian was killed and another wounded when they were caught by timber cutters on the Rio Branco.

• In November 1989, federal police recovered the bodies of three Korubo believed to have been hunted down and murdered by timber cutters.

• In November 1991, two men working for the SHEM timber company in Korubo lands went missing. The company dispatched ten armed men to find them and, according to the Catholic Church's Indigenous Commission, punished the Indians believed responsible for their deaths (*Porantim,* December 1991).

• On the 28th March 1988, 14 Ticuna Indians, children included, were killed and 22 wounded in an attack by timber cutter Oscar Castello Branco and sixteen hired gunmen (*Jornal do Brasil* 8.4.88, *Mensageiro* No. 68, March/April 1991). Despite being named as the instigator of the massacre by the director-general of the Federal Police in Brazil, neither Branco nor any of the gunmen have been prosecuted.

• There have been constant battles between the loggers and the Surui of Rondonia. In October 1988 the Surui, Cinta Larga, Arara, Gaviao and Zoro tied up 6 timber workers they found on the Surui reserve and threatened to kill them (Verissimo 1992). In 1989, one of the Surui men opposed to the logging disappeared, believed killed (*Correio Braziliense* 1.2.89). In October 1991, 400 Indians blocked the main bridge of Ji-Parana to protest against dams, ranching, mining and timber cutting on indigenous lands (*Porantim,* November 1991).

• In September 1990, gunmen hired by timber companies murdered two of the isolated Awa-Guaja Indians in the Gurupi Biological Reserve. There are 80 armed men hired by the timber cutters and ranchers operating in the Biological Reserve (*Mensageiro* No. 67, January/February 1991).

• In the Sakurap-Makurap reserve, Rondonia, Indians confiscated logging vehicles. On Christmas Day 1991, 26 armed men hired by a timber cutter raided a Sakirabiar community to recover the logging vehicles the Indians had confiscated. In reprisals, logging company gunmen took hostages and shot one man in the head (*Porantim,* January/February 1992).

• In February 1991, after timber cutters had ignored repeated requests

by the Cinta Larga in Rondonia to leave their lands, 35 Indian men sur-
rounded five of the workers and killed them. In October 1988, the 70-
year-old Zoro chief Yaminer was kidnapped by timber cutters and shot
dead. His body was burned and left beside a road. Four illegal timber cutters were later charged with murder (*Jornal do Brasil* 26.10.88, *Correio
Braziliense* 4.11.88).

Loggers' tactics against local Indians

1. In some cases, mahogany cutters move into the reserve clandestinely,
cutting until the Indians discover them. At that point they either leave,
threaten the Indians or try to suborn them.

2. In the territories of people such as the Kayapo, renowned for their
violent resistance to timber cutting, loggers have been known to dash in,
fell as many mahogany trees as they can, then approach the Indians
through intermediaries, arguing that as the wood has already been felled,
the Indians can only gain by receiving a share of the profits once the logs
are hauled away and sawn.

3. Cutters distribute truckloads of cheap merchandise: torches [flash-
lights], radios, T-shirts, biscuits and tinned food. A few weeks later they
return, claiming that the goods had been sold to the Indians on credit,
and that they have come to collect their debts in the form of timber.

4. The cutters single out members of the group and attempt to per-
suade them of the merits of trading their timber. If they succeed, contracts are drawn up. These are both illegal and, characteristically, one-
sided. The Indians are paid in cash, services or merchandise, at rates far
below those charged by other landowners. Even so, cutters often steal
more wood than they pay for.

The vast majority of mahogany is illegally logged.

According to Jose Lutzenberger and other government sources, the
majority of Brazil's mahogany exports have been illegally logged in Indian and biological reserves (Lutzenberger 1992).

The Brazilian Constitution determines that "the lands traditionally
occupied by the Indians are set aside for their permanent possession, leaving to them the exclusive use of the riches from the soil, the rivers and
the lakes existing in them" (Senado Federal 1988). Not only are the logging activities in demarcated Indian territory without Indian permission
illegal, but, under Brazilian law, any logging by non-Indians in indigenous reserves must be approved by the National Congress. Not one such
logging operation ever has been submitted for approval, and no timber
on the export market is known to come from Indian controlled operations. Therefore ALL timber currently coming from Indian lands is illegal.

The current logging is also breaking the Brazilian Statute of the Indian and the Draft United Nations Declaration on the Rights of Indigenous Peoples International Labour Organization's Conventions 107 and
169 (Monbiot 1992).

In 1987 the Brazilian export agency, CACEX, recorded that 69% of all
the mahogany leaving Brazil came from the Kayapo reserves (CEDI 1992).
This proportion has since declined due to depletion. In 1988 the ex-
director of FUNAI, Ezequias Heringuer Filho, reported that a preliminary
study in Rondonia, Mato Grosso, Amazonas and Para showed that at least

$1 billion worth of timber had already been removed from indigenous reserves (*Diario* 1988). Illegal mahogany logging is also taking part in biological and extractive reserves (Ecopore 1991).

Loggers are bribing officials.

Many of the civil servants charged with protecting the Indians and the forests, as well as members of the judiciary, have been bribed or threatened into acquiescence with the illegal trade. Some officials are known to draw regular salaries from the loggers (Lutzenberger 1992, Sydney Possuelo, President of FUNAI, pers. comm., FUNAI officials, Para, pers. comm., cited in Monbiot 1992). Jose Lutzenberger, the former Brazilian secretary for the environment, described IBAMA, the Brazilian Environment Department, as being "just another branch of the logging industry . . . a den of crooks and thieves" (*Washington Post*, March 21, 1992).

In an open letter to British consumers, Lutzenberger says:

> Though timber cutting inside reserves is illegal, timber traders in many parts of the Amazon wield more money and power than most government departments. They have succeeded in corrupting many of the people charged with the protection of the Indians and Forests. My attempts to stop their illegal activities were partly responsible for my sacking (Lutzenberger 1992).

Loggers are ignoring forestry law.

The Brazilian Department of Forests clearly has no real control over logging. There are only 50 forest rangers to monitor the entire Amazon and most concessions are probably never inspected.

Although government fines for illegal cutting can, in theory, be as high as US $1,200 per ha [hectare], these have not been enforced. Indeed, in some areas, the majority of logging is totally illegal and operating without any permit. In Acre, for example, 400,000 ha of forest were logged although only 100,000 ha had been allocated for logging (Plowden, Kusada 1989). In September 1988 one representative of the government exported 22,000 m³ [cubic meters] of unprocessed mahogany logs from Itacoatiara to China. The declarations were false and made through a 'front company' (Pabst undated).

There have been a large number of cases of Indians being murdered by timber cutters.

In theory, operations should be issued with management certificates by the federal Environment Department, IBAMA, as proof of good management practices. However, these have long been an object of ridicule among researchers in the Amazon. In 1992 Jose Lutzenberger revealed that they were being handed out blank by corrupt IBAMA officials for the cutters to fill in for themselves (Monbiot 1992).

The Brazilian Department of Forests required logging companies to pay a reforestation tax of 62 cruzados/tree (October 1988 rate). In reality it has done no reforestation with this income, and has used the money elsewhere (Pabst undated).

Loggers are breaking contract law.

Although there are no specific laws regulating contracts with tribal groups, such contracts are invalid under general contract law requiring that all parties have a full understanding of the terms of the contract being signed. The Indians' lack of understanding of the meaning or contents of contracts has also been exploited by companies. According to Kayapo spokesman Paulinho Paiakan, "At the moment, very few of us can speak or read Portuguese. Fewer even can count or check money deals. Numbers are not part of our tradition. We were always cheated" (Paiakan 1992).

When contracts have been signed with local Indians it has invariably been with a very few individuals with no authority to represent the entire tribal group, such as in the Kayapo contract with Maginco (Vidal and Giannini 1992) or by FUNAI acting on the Indians' behalf. Romero Juca' Filho, head of FUNAI from 1986 to 1991, signed many such contracts on behalf of the Indians resulting in huge personal gains for himself (*Senhor* 20.10.87). He also reached deals with logging companies to construct the FUNAI administrative buildings in reserves, thus reducing FUNAI overheads. These contracts caused a national scandal and were canceled by the federal courts in 1988 (*Correio Braziliense*, 6.8.88) but the cutters continued to use them in attempts to legitimise their presence.

In some areas, the majority of logging is totally illegal and operating without any permit.

Although Sydney Possuelo, Filho's successor at FUNAI, is determined to stop the abuses, middle-ranking officials throughout the foundation continue to preside over contracts between cutters and Indians, taking a substantial cut from the loggers in return for convincing the Indians that they are not being treated unfairly (Monbiot 1992).

Breaking tax law.

Mahogany companies have been grossly underdeclaring their level of cutting to avoid paying tax. In Para state, the main source of mahogany, companies declared to the Department of Forests that they had cut only 2,174,715 cubic meters. In reality they had cut 39,803,595 cubic meters, nearly 20 times as much. The level of tax defraudation is 94.5% (Greenpeace 1992).

Virtually nothing has been done to stop these illegal activities.

In the very few cases where FUNAI or the police have attempted to enforce the law, they have been virtually powerless against the loggers. In every case where the logging has been temporarily stopped, the companies have simply started again.

A case in point was the 1991 application by FUNAI to the Federal Attorney-General of Para against Bannach's illegal operations in the Arara-Xingu catchment. The judge made a preliminary measure which he subsequently withdrew (Potiguar 1991).

In Guapore, Rondonia, there were four expeditions mounted by FUNAI, some with the help of the federal police, to close down the timber operations in the reserve by the middle of 1991. After every expedition the cutters began operating almost immediately, relying on the widespread support of corrupt officials. In the dry season of 1991 a more effective operation was launched, which stopped the cutting in the reserve at least until the end of that year (Monbiot 1992).

On January 15th, 1993, Selene Maria de Almeida, a judge in the Brasilia Federal Court, placed an immediate interdiction on all illegal roads being opened by logging companies in demarcated indigenous lands in South Para. The companies named included Perachi and Maginco, two of the largest suppliers to the UK market (see below). They were given 10 days to stop all road building activities and withdraw all equipment and employees. Only Perachi is appealing the decision.

The role of the British

Britain is the world's largest market for mahogany. In 1990, Britain imported 62,000 tonnes of sawn Brazilian mahogany, 74% of the mahogany entering Europe, and 52% of Brazilian exports. Only 20% of Brazilian mahogany is consumed in Brazil, making Britain the largest consumer in the world (Monbiot 1992).

Given this overwhelming importance of Britain to the Brazilian mahogany industry, a fall in UK demand would have a dramatic effect on the Brazilian industry, especially as mahogany has no significant Brazilian market.

The main benefactors of the Brazilian mahogany trade are the intermediaries, who take 80% of the price, and the UK government, which collects VAT [value-added tax] on the sale price. Johnson (1991) estimates that the British government earns twice as much per cubic meter on VAT as the Brazilian logging company which produced it. Francesco Martone of Greenpeace International suggests that the VAT on Brazilian mahogany alone may well exceed the British Overseas Development Administration's spending in 1990/91 on all forestry projects (Martone 1991).

According to the International Tropical Timber Organisation (ITTO) the Brazilian forest sector is 4% of GNP and creates 60,000 direct and 300,000 indirect jobs. Thirty-three percent production directly consumed in the Amazonian states, 55% for other parts of Brazil, 12% for export (cited Plowden, Kusada 1989). This means that only 7,200 people are involved directly in timber production for export. Given that mahogany was only a third of exports in 1990 (Hahn 1991), this would mean that only 2,376 people are directly employed and 11,880 indirectly employed in the mahogany industry.

British companies are buying mahogany from the worst Brazilian companies. The following is detailed evidence of illegal practices by three of the main companies supplying the UK with Brazilian mahogany; Maginco, Bannach and Parachi, which are understood to supply two-thirds of the UK mahogany market (T. Mallinson, pers. comm.). In November 1992, Dr. Sydney Possuelo of FUNAI challenged the British timber companies to stop buying mahogany from just these three companies, which, he said, were all involved in illegal activities. Since then, Maginco and Perachi have been found guilty of illegal logging by the Brazilian federal courts. All three are known to have direct links with British importers and wholesalers. The following British companies have admitted in writing or on film to buying from these companies:

- Timbmet: Perachi, Bannach, Maginco
- Burbidge: Maginco
- M & N Norman: Maginco
- Latham's: Maginco
- 10 Downing St.: Maginco
- Buck. Palace: Maginco
- Hunters: Perachi

M & N Norman, the main supplier of mahogany to Scotland, and Richard Burbidge now claim to have ceased buying mahogany from Brazil. It is believed, though, that Richard Burbidge has continued to sell mahogany to his wholesale customers. In a reply to a House of Commons question in 1989, then Prime Minister Margaret Thatcher confirmed that 25 m£ [million British pounds] of Brazilian mahogany used to refurbish rooms in 10 Downing Street was bought from Maginco (*Hansard* 1989). Mahogany for the restoration of Buckingham Palace was purchased from Latham's, which has admitted that 95% of its supplies come from Maginco.

Logging companies and indigenous groups

The following is from Vidal, Giannini 1992 and *Aconteceu* 24.1.92.

The Xikrin. In 1991 alone, logging companies extracted 30,000 cubic meters of mahogany illegally from the Xikrin lands in Catete. In July 1989, Bannach Industria persuaded two co-opted Xikrin leaders to sign a contract allowing it to cut 20,000 m³ per year for five years. Bannach got 50% of the wood in payment for its services, with the Xikrin obliged to sell it the remainder for $100 per 5 trees. The market price in 1989 for standing mahogany trees in the region was $80 per cubic meter: an average of $230 per tree.

The regional administrator of FUNAI, Jose Ferreira Campos, Junior, said, "The cynicism of this contract is such that 50% of the wood extracted goes to the company to pay for its own extradition of the wood. . . . It's the first time that I've seen a timber company being paid for extracting timber."

The money was not delivered to the Indians. On the contract, a debt of $7900 owed by the Xikrin to Bannach appears spent on "merchandise" for the Xikrin. At the end of 1990 the Xikrin, finding that they had received almost nothing in return for their wood, tried to get the contract annulled. Certain that nothing would be done, Bannach resumed logging in July 1990, offering the Xikrin a twin motored airplane and a road linking their village to Tucuma. Bannach contracted a further 5 companies to accelerate the cutting. Perachi was one of these companies.

In September 1990, Mr. Bannach accosted the local head of FUNAI and told him, "Money pays for anything, and the federal police will not enter the Xikrin area and you will never succeed in opening an inquiry about me."

There is reported to be widespread alcoholism, prostitution and venereal diseases, and social breakdown as the leaders lose control of the community and the young people break away with easy money. According to Isabelle Giannini, in the first 2 weeks of 1992, 6 Xikrin children died of viral dysentery.

Parakana and Arawete Indians. Perachi and Maginco have been working inside the Arawete and Apytera reserves of the Parakana and Arawete Indians since 1988 and constructed a 240 km road, which is now the launch pad of further invasions. Before being discovered by the Indians in April 1988, these companies extracted 7,500 m^3 of illegal mahogany. Two anthropologists working with the Parakana Indians reported that two representatives of Maginco were in the village of the Parakana in March 1992, offering the Indians many presents in return for timber rights.

They write:

> We are witnessing a brutal and immoral process of bribery of an indigenous population of recent contact, without any capacity for defense. . . . Maginco is buying the Parakana, because until now it has not succeeded in "negotiating" to their content with FUNAI. It is a new method, but the results are the same: Indians humiliated, land (still not fully demarcated) degraded, creation of needs which the Indians could never satisfy, despoliation of natural resources and, it is clear, enrichment of the timber companies and pretty mahogany furniture in Europe.

The Kayapo. Maginco is one of four companies operating illegally in Kayapo territory. According to FUNAI figures, it extracted 4,432 logs in 1988. In 1992 Kayapo leaders complained that the remotest of their forests—the territory of the Pukanu community—were invaded by Maginco. Maginco was well aware that the people of that community were opposed to any deals with timber cutters, and were likely to resist them with violence. It carried out a 'lightning strike', invading the reserve and felling as many mahogany trees as possible in the space of a few weeks. It then sent an intermediary to negotiate with the Pukanu community, arguing that as the wood had already been cut, the Kayapo had nothing to lose by allowing Maginco to remove it in exchange for money (Kayapo leader on visit to UK, April 1992).

There is reported to be widespread alcoholism, prostitution and venereal diseases, and social breakdown [among indigenous populations].

The Arara/Xingu. The Arara Indians of the Xingu catchment were first contracted by the Brazilian government in 1981 and fled from the lands the company entered, moving to the far west of their territory. In 1991 Bannach built a 95 km logging road westwards, which came to within 20 km of the western Arara's new village, and built a sawmill on the banks of the River Iriri. Fifteen hundred families of colonists followed the timber cutters, settling along the main road and the smaller ones it built. One of the companies involved is owned by a government agency, INCRA, which is cutting the mahogany for use by a timber company belonging to one of its senior officials (*O Liberal* 10.11.88).

As the colonists following the timber company have clear-felled a wide track of forest which the Arara cannot cross, the 38 people surviving

in the western territories have no means of contacting the larger populations in the east. Their total population is believed to have fallen to
around one quarter of the pre-contact number and they are said to be suffering from flu epidemics.

References

Aconteceu. Publication of the Centro Ecumenico de Documentacao e Infor-
macao, São Paulo.

Albrechtsen, 1991. Cited in de Barros 1992.

Bannach, 1991. *Letter to FW Morley and Sons,* Madeireira Bannach Ltda.

de Barros, P.L.C. et al., 1992. *Natural and Artificial Reserves of Swietenia macrophylla, King in the Brazilian Amazon—a Perspective for Conservation.* MS.
Belém, Para.

Campbell, Faith, 1992. *CITES Proposal to put American mahogonies, genus
Swietenia, in Appendix II,* Natural Resources Defense Council, 9.1.92.

Campbell, Faith, 1992. *Summary of the Timber Issues at the Conference of the Parties to CITES,* Natural Resources Defense Council, Washington, 2–13th
March.

CEDI, 1992. *Povos indigenas no Brasil 1987/88/89/90. Aconteceu Especial* 18.

Correio Braziliense, Brasilia.

Diario do Grande ABC, 8.9.88. São Paulo.

Ecopore, 1991. *Simposio: Madeiras e mine'rios em areas de preservacao perma-
nente.* Acao Ecologica Vale do Guapore.

Fausto, Carlos, 1992. In CEDI : 1992.

Greenpeace, 1992. *Predatory Mahogany Logging: A Threat to the Future of the
Amazon.* MS. Greenpeace Brazil, Rio de Janeiro.

Hahn, L., 1991. *Amazonian Wood Exports,* Greenpeace Brazil. MS.

Hansard, 1989. *Question by Kirkwood MP to PM,* 20.6.89. Victoria, British Columbia.

Informe Juri'dico, 1991. Publication of the Comissao Pro Indio São Paulo, No.
17, August.

Johnson, B., 1991. *The Value of Tropical Timber and Who Benefits from It,* World
Wildlife Fund United Kingdom. MS.

Jornal do Brasil, Rio de Janeiro.

Lamb, F.B., 1966. *Mahogany of Tropical America: Its Ecology and Management.*
University of Michigan Press, Ann Arbor.

Lutzenberger, Jose, 1992. *Open Letter to British Consumers,* Porto Alegre, April
30.

Martone, F., 1991. *Tropical Timber Imports from Brazil into the European Community,* Greenpeace International Tropical Forests Campaign.

Mensageiro. Publication of the Conselho Indigenista Missionario, Belém.

Monbiot, George, 1991. "Against the Grain," *The Guardian,* Friday, May 3.

Monbiot, George, 1992. *Mahogany Is Murder,* Friends of the Earth, London.

Montagner, Delvair, 1992. In CEDI.

O Liberal, Belém, Para. 10.11.88.

Pabst, Eije, undated. *Timber export from Brazil—first result.* MS.

Padua, J.A., Anderson, P., 1992. *Deforestation in Brazil, Causes and Cures,* 27.5.92, Greenpeace International.

Paiakan, Paulinho, 1992. *Letter to the Bodyshop.* 19.3.92.

Plowden, C., Kusada, Y., 1989. *Logging in the Brazilian Rainforest,* Terra international, Washington. Rainforest Alliance Workshop, New York.

Porantim, Conselho Indigenista Misionario, Brasilia.

Potiguar, J.A.T., 1991. *Application to Federal Judge Daniel Paes Ribeiro,* 4th Federal Judiciary District, Para.

Rasmusson, U., 1989. *Comments vis-a-vis the World Bank load for "Rondonia Natural Resource Management,"* World Wildlife Fund Sweden 20.12.89.

Rasmusson, U., 1989a. *Travel report from visits to the state of Rondonia, Brazil.* MS. Friends of the Earth, Sweden.

Senado Federal, 1988. *Constituicao,* Republica Federativa do Brasil. Article 231.

Senhor, São Paulo.

Styles, B.T., 1981. *Swietenioideae.* In Pennington, T.D., Styles, Meliaceae : 359–418. New York Botanical Garden. New York.

Survival International, 1991. *Urgent Action Bulletin.* "Uru Eu Wau Wau Population Halved. Remainder Face Genocide."

Uhl, Christopher et al., 1990. *Wood as an Economic Catalyst to Ecological Change in Amazonia.* MS. Cited Monbiot 1990. Original unseen.

Uhl, Christopher, undated. *Aging of the Amazon Frontier. Opportunities for Genuine Development,* Pennsylvania State Univ. MS.

Verissimo, A., et al., 1992. *Mahogany extraction in the eastern Amazon: a case study.* MS.

Vidal, L. and Giannini, I., 1992. *Povos indigenas no Brasil 1987/88/89/90. Aconteceu Especial* 18. CEDI.

4

Logging Is a Threat to British Columbia's Rainforests

Raincoast Conservation Society

Raincoast Conservation Society is a Canadian organization in Victoria, British Columbia, that opposes the logging of British Columbia's temperate rainforests.

Logging threatens to destroy much of British Columbia's temperate rainforest wilderness and reduce the number of animals that depend on this habitat to survive. Salmon, other fishes, and grizzly bears are among the wildlife endangered by continued rainforest logging.

Editor's note: The rainforest wilderness systems described in the following viewpoint have subsequently been combined under one name: The Great Bear Rainforest.

Obscured by coastal fog and hidden in the shadows of glacier-capped mountains, the Canadian Raincoast Wilderness contains a significant portion of all remaining temperate rainforest in the world. Extending from Knight Inlet north to Alaska, this is a rain-drenched biologically diverse wilderness where grizzly bears typically saunter through ancient forests of cedar and spruce to reach estuaries swarming with salmon.

But few people are aware of this unique ecoregion, and the British Columbia government has protected almost none of this ancient rainforest landscape.

In the meantime, commercial clearcutting and overfishing are destroying the rainforest ecosystems.

Wildlife habitat continues to disappear, and every year there are fewer grizzlies and fewer salmon, just as there are fewer old-growth cedar and spruce.

Much of the old-growth forest of the raincoast wilderness already has

From the Raincoast Conservation Society report, "Canadian Raincoast Wilderness," at http://vanbc.wimsey.com/~erich/rancoast/rancoast.html, June 18, 1997, revised by Peter McAllister, president, September 16, 1997. Reprinted with permission.

been logged. But the opportunity still remains to protect a large segment of this temperate rainforest, to establish wilderness reserves on a grand scale.

Out of a broad coastal landscape of some seven million hectares, the Raincoast Conservation Society has identified for protection three wilderness rainforest regions [described later] covering roughly three million hectares (1 hectare = 2.47 acres).

The wilderness landscape

There are few towns of any size along the mainland coast of British Columbia, but half a dozen small Native communities lie tucked away in select coastal locations.

They remind us that this rainforest wilderness is the homeland of a number of First Nations, including those who reside today in the coastal villages of Bella Bella, Bella Coola, Hartley Bay, Kitimat Village, Port Simpson and Klemtu.

The world these First Nations inhabit is highlighted by a labyrinth of deep-water fiords and a maze of offshore islands. It is a roadless world where granite peaks shoot straight out of the ocean.

Corridors of coastal rainforest—primarily western hemlock, Pacific silver fir, Sitka spruce, yellow cedar and western red cedar—grow along the low-lying valleys of winding inlets and rivers. The outer coastal islands are often carpeted in muskeg.

This is a wilderness rich in wildlife where grizzlies, black bears and wolves predominate. A rare, snow-white color variation of the black bear, the Kermode, hides in isolated coastal wilderness pockets.

Wild salmon abound in the ocean waters; some 800–1,000 coastal rivers are home to spawning salmon. Many other rivers have evolved unique varieties of land-locked trout and salmon.

Much of the life of the rainforest revolves around these nutrient-rich rivers and streams. Wildlife of every kind congregate here; the stream-side forests produce some of the finest tree specimens of the temperate rainforest.

Yet, in the broad rugged landscape of the Canadian Raincoast Wilderness, as little as 10 percent of the land supports trees of commercial size. Consequently, protecting all remaining low-elevation rainforest corridors is absolutely essential to the overall protection of the coastal temperate rainforest.

Almost every wilderness valley or inlet with significant stands of timber will have logging roads through it before the year 2000.

There are some 200 primary watersheds along the British Columbia mainland coast greater than 5,000 hectares. About 60 of these are still largely undeveloped.

But the B.C. coast also includes hundreds of smaller watersheds, many of which are still intact. Each of these valleys is a masterpiece of nature, and much of the ecological value of the region is tied up in these smaller river systems.

The trees of this raincoast wilderness grow on public (Crown) forest land, and the British Columbia Ministry of Forests is intent on clearcutting almost all of them.

Many of the better quality, low-elevation forests have now been clearcut. Almost every wilderness valley or inlet with significant stands of timber will have logging roads through it before the year 2000. Most of the remaining marketable timber is slated to be logged in the next two decades.

Biological diversity and abundance is under severe threat today from commercial logging, overfishing, and even salmon enhancement projects.

Once that happens, the entire rainforest ecosystem will be left in ruin.

Temperate rainforests—predominantly evergreen forests that receive at least 1,016 millimetres (40 inches) of rain a year over a minimum of 100 days—are extremely rare in the world. Two-thirds of these globally unique ecosystems occur along the west coast of North America.

Extending south from Alaska down the coast of British Columbia to Washington and Oregon, these temperate rainforests often surpass tropical rainforests in tree size and total forest biomass. The dominant trees easily live from 300 to 800 years; some grow to be much older. The ecosystem is characterized by a wide range of tree sizes and ages, and a many-layered canopy.

The largest concentration of these ancient temperate rainforests is found in British Columbia, where they divide into two distinct parts—the southern and northern forests.

Logging in the south has gone on for more than a century, and only a handful of southern rainforest watersheds were ever protected. (For example, only six percent of Vancouver Island's fabled ancient rainforest has been saved.)

The northern rainforest, nestled in a remote and mountainous landscape, has been much less developed—until now.

To adequately conserve the full range of biological diversity and wilderness values found in the ancient temperate rainforest of the mainland coast of British Columbia, Canada, the Raincoast Conservation Society has identified three major, ecologically rich wilderness areas that must be permanently protected from commercial logging:

- The Great Bear Wilderness System
- The Greater Ecstall Wilderness System
- The Greater Khutzeymateen Wilderness System

The vanishing salmon

The wild salmon of the raincoast face mass extinction. Forty years of stream-by-stream observations in a thousand salmon spawning rivers by Canada's Department of Fisheries and Oceans, together with four years of field work by the Raincoast Conservation Society, has confirmed the

worst—the overall numbers of wild coho, sockeye, chinook, and sometimes chum and pink salmon have declined sharply over the decades.

In a large number of the approximately 90 rivers visited by the Raincoast Conservation Society, the wild coho appear to have all but vanished.

It is unlikely that populations of chinook, steelhead and cut-throat
have fared any better.

Over millions of years, perhaps a thousand races of wild salmon have
evolved as unique runs in the rivers of the Canadian Raincoast. Along
with the bear, the wolf and the eagle, an extraordinary profusion of
aquatic and terrestrial life forms owe their existence to the annual ritual
of spawning salmon. For thousands of years, salmon have nurtured and
enriched the life and culture of the First Nations.

This biological diversity and abundance is under severe threat today
from commercial logging, overfishing, and even salmon enhancement
projects.

Commercial logging in coastal watersheds continues to destroy
salmon habitat. Spawning beds are smothered with sediment, nutrient
cycles are disrupted and rivers are gouged and destabilized.

---

*As the rainforest enclaves are systematically clearcut,
the entire wilderness ecosystem slowly unravels.*

Overfishing of wild salmon stocks, together with one hundred years
of inadequate government management, are the principal documented
causes of salmon decline. Less well known are the negative effects of artificially replacing and boosting salmon runs with fish hatcheries and
salmon enhancement programs. These are unsustainable, enormously
costly and biologically unsound. As well, wild salmon often get inter-
cepted in fish harvests that target artificially reared salmon.

The protection of the surviving wild salmon of the raincoast is an international conservation priority. The remaining unlogged watersheds
must be turned into fish and wildlife sanctuaries, and clearcut valleys
must be restored to ecological health.

The vanishing grizzly

No one can say for sure how many grizzlies currently roam British
Columbia's Coastal rainforests. Estimates have run between 1,000 and
2,000. But one thing is known for sure; there are considerably fewer grizzly bears today than there used to be.

A male grizzly on the coast is likely to range across a series of wild river
valleys, but its main habitat is the low-elevation temperate rainforest. A fe-
male grizzly may live out her life in just one or two wilderness watersheds.

History shows that when logging roads are pushed into a forest wilderness, grizzly bears inevitably disappear. Their denning sites are destroyed,
their food supply is disrupted and they are more easily hunted down.

Grizzlies need old-growth forests to survive. Many large coastal valleys that once supported grizzly bears have been logged today, and the
grizzlies are disappearing.

Current efforts to protect grizzlies are meagre at best. What is required are large, salmon-rich, wilderness watershed reserves that protect the full range of grizzly bear habitat, especially old-growth forests and forest streams that are so critical to the survival of wildlife and fish.

The health of the grizzly bear populations is a direct reflection of the health of the Canadian Raincoast Wilderness.

Conserving wilderness systems

If logging continues as planned in the central and north coasts of British Columbia, within a decade the best remaining forests and the best remaining fish and wildlife habitat throughout the ecosystem will be destroyed.

The situation has been made worse by British Columbia's 1995 forest practices code. Little more than a public relations exercise, the code is used by the British Columbian government to disguise ongoing destructive clearcut logging. Under the code, logging companies are encouraged to disperse their clearcuts more rapidly through the remaining wild rainforest valleys.

There is an urgent need to protect the key components of the Canadian Raincoast Wilderness—especially all unlogged, low-elevation and streamside forests.

The B.C. government announced plans to protect the Kitlope and Khutzeymateen valleys of the north coast. Yet on their own, the Kitlope and the Khutzeymateen protect only a small fraction of the coastal temperate rainforest and wildlife habitat. Certainly, grizzlies found in these valleys also travel through neighboring, unprotected watersheds.

A truly effective wilderness protection program must link together a series of intact rainforest watersheds, including their marine estuaries. This will provide the only true protection for the coastal temperate rainforest, the salmon, the grizzly bear and all the other fish and wildlife still thriving in such a spectacular natural system.

While as little as 10 percent of the Canadian Raincoast Wilderness supports commercial-scale forests—the rest of the landscape is dominated by water, rock and muskeg—these forests grow in the region's most biologically productive environments. As the rainforest enclaves are systematically clearcut, the entire wilderness ecosystem slowly unravels.

Three wilderness areas

To adequately conserve the full range of biological diversity in this wilderness region of some seven million hectares, the Raincoast Conservation Society has roughly defined three major, ecologically rich wilderness areas totalling three million hectares that must be permanently protected from commercial logging.

The Great Bear Wilderness System (2.3 million hectares).

Dubbed "the little Amazon," the Great Bear Wilderness area is the heartland of British Columbia's ancient temperate rainforest. Including the magnificent landscape of the Kitlope Valley and the ancient temperate rainforests surrounding Princess Royal Channel, Roscoe Inlet and Ellerslie Lake, this is a wilderness maze of granite-rimmed fiords and narrow inlets lined with old-growth forests. The links of land and sea are very strong here, making this area rich in fish and wildlife, and the core region for ecological diversity in the Canadian Raincoast Wilderness.

The Greater Ecstall Wilderness System (400,000 hectares).

The Greater Ecstall Wilderness System is largely a daunting landscape of rock and ice penetrated from all sides by finger-like, pristine, wonderfully scenic river valleys. The Ecstall watershed itself, like the Kitlope, is one of the last remaining very large, but still very wild, river systems in the Canadian Raincoast Wilderness.

The Greater Khutzeymateen Wilderness System (250,000 hectares).

This is the northern range of the Canadian Raincoast Wilderness, where the Coast Mountains tower over narrow, meandering, tree-lined river valleys. Commercial logging operations surround this wilderness system that is centred around the already protected Khutzeymateen Valley. If logging spreads into the remaining wilderness watersheds, the ecological integrity of the entire region—including the Khutzeymateen—will be undermined.

This conservation proposal will continue to be updated as more is learned about the largely unstudied environments of the Canadian Raincoast Wilderness.

5

Tropical Deforestation Is a Health Threat

Roger L. Shapiro

Roger L. Shapiro was an intern in internal medicine at Beth Israel Hospital in Boston when this article was originally published.

The loss of rainforests and their plant species could seriously affect human health and endanger lives. Many valuable pharmaceuticals are derived from rainforest plants. Tropical plants also play an important role in sustaining the nutritional diversity of food crops for human consumption. Preserving rainforests can prevent flooding, soil erosion, and the spread of diseases such as malaria.

As the twenty-first century approaches, the role of the physician continues to expand. Health issues, population pressures, and environmental problems have begun to merge on both a local and global level, and this process will accelerate in the coming years. A 1992 World Health Organization [WHO] report states that "human health is a vital cross-sectoral issue, dependent on the continued availability of environmental resources and on the integrity of the environment." The report also calls for all health professionals to assume a central role in the process of environmental protection [1].

Here tropical deforestation is examined as it affects human health. Although many environmental issues are associated with significant health problems, the consequences of deforestation alone sufficiently serve to exemplify how health issues and environmental degradation are inextricably bound. Deforestation, particularly in the world's tropical rain forests, has both an indirect and direct impact on human health. The loss of biodiversity as a result of deforestation has far-reaching ethical, medicinal and agricultural, and ecological implications, and a deforested landscape contributes directly to human disease through change in disease vectors and influence on urbanization and poverty.

Conversion to agricultural and grazing land, as well as commercial and local logging operations, have the largest impact on global deforestation. In the tropics, 60% of deforestation results from new agricultural

From Roger L. Shapiro, "The Effects of Tropical Deforestation on Human Health," *PSR Quarterly*, vol. 3, no. 3, September 1993. Copyright 1993 BMJ Publishing Group. Reprinted by permission of *PSR Quarterly*, now known as *Medicine and Global Survival*.

settlements, and in all developing countries, logging represents nearly 20% of forest loss. Unfortunately, less than 1% of tropical logging operations are sustainably managed, and logging roads allow farmers and grazers access to new areas of the forest [2]. Poverty and population pressure lie beneath the surface causes of worldwide deforestation. A Brazilian farmer will resort to slash and burn agriculture to feed his family, even though nutrient-poor rain forest soil remains productive for only a few years. Similarly, Somalis will scour a barren landscape for scraps of firewood when that wood is their last remaining asset.

On the basis of satellite data and ground estimates, a reasonable figure for tropical rain forest loss in 1989 was 1.8% per year. These forests currently cover about half of their prehistoric area, and this rate of loss would again cut their area in half by the year 2022. According to an estimate by Harvard biologist E.O. Wilson, surviving tropical rain forests in 1989 occupied an area approximately equal to the continental United States, and the area disappearing each year was roughly the size of Florida [3]. Outside the tropics, many of the world's other forests have fared no better. In Nepal, half of the forest cover has been lost in the last decade, and population pressure and poverty in India threaten to destroy all of its remaining forests by the turn of the century [4,5].

Deforestation and biodiversity loss

The issue of biodiversity loss is intimately connected with deforestation, especially in tropical rain forests. Habitat destruction is by far the leading mechanism of extinction, and conservative calculations estimate that one half of all species exist solely in tropical forests [6]. The most serious problem facing scientists attempting to quantify species loss is that we simply do not know how many species exist. There are currently about 1.4 million named species on the planet, but most estimates place the true number between 5 and 30 million [6]. At the present rate of deforestation and the conservative estimate of 10 million rain forest species, Wilson estimates that between 10% and 22% of species in the rain forest may become extinct in the next thirty years, representing between 5% and 10% of the total species on Earth. This rate is equivalent to a loss of approximately three species per hour [6]. The World Commission on Environment and Development, in its landmark book *Our Common Future,* further estimates that at 1987 deforestation rates, 15% of all plant species will become extinct by the year 2000, and that without the creation of new reserves or a change in this trend, up to 66% of all plant species and 69% of all bird species will eventually be lost [7].

These estimates of species loss are conservative. They are based on area estimates alone, which do not account for specialization and localization of species within rain forests, and they do not account for the weakening of species by reduced genetic variation among survivors. Furthermore, the potential change in rain forest ecosystems due to deforestation is not addressed. For example, loss of half the forest might well reduce the remaining half to an open woodland because of an inability to maintain enough moisture [6]. This process, combined with human pressures on selected species and the encroachment of "common" weeds and animals from adjacent regions, may drive up the extinction rate even further. On the basis of Thomas Lovejoy's Minimum Critical Size of Ecosystems Project in Brazil, E.O. Wilson concludes that "an Amazon forest chopped into many small fragments will become no more than a skeleton of its former self" [3,7].

Between 10% and 22% of species in the rain forest may become extinct in the next thirty years.

Critics of these statistics state that we do not have precise information about the number of species in the rain forests or a model reliable enough to make such grim predictions. Ariel Lugo of the Institute of Tropical Forestry in Puerto Rico points out the resiliency of many tropical ecosystems and notes that following massive deforestation diversity has returned to islands like Puerto Rico, leading to the creation of new "native" plants. Others contend, however, that this represents the secondary invasion of common "tramp" species and not a true return of biodiversity [8,9]. The most challenging and pervasive of all arguments against acting to prevent tropical deforestation is: "So what?" In the last 500 million years there have been five mass extinctions on the planet, and about 99% of all species that have ever existed are now extinct. What, one might ask, is the danger? To address this question, an obvious starting point is the fossil record, which indicates that following each of those periods it took tens of millions of years for diversity to return to pre-extinction levels. Modern *Homo sapiens* have existed for less than 100,000 years, and our tenure may not extend into the millions. Thus, as humans accelerate the process of extinction on the planet, we condemn our future generations to a more isolated—and perhaps precarious—existence. Another consideration is the current speed and scope of species loss due to human activity; it is estimated to have increased the baseline extinction rate in tropical rain forests between 1,000 and 10,000 times [3]. These figures demand our attention and deny us the comfort of historical precedent. As we remodel the planet in the blink of an eye by geological time, and as we create the environment of our descendants, we relinquish the right to say "so what" or to throw our arms skyward and ask, "why?" The responsibility for the changes lies with us.

In their 1991 article "Biodiversity Studies: Science and Policy," Paul Ehrlich and E.O. Wilson outline three reasons why everyone should be concerned with the loss of biodiversity: 1) ethical and esthetic reasons, 2) economic benefits in the form of medicine and food, and 3) the essential services provided by natural ecosystems [10]. Each of these reasons has significant implications for human health, as will become more clear in the following discussion.

Ethics

The ethical and esthetic arguments for species protection run deep, particularly for physicians. The process of human evolution involved (and involves) complex interactions with the other species on Earth; all of our instincts, all of our patterns of behavior, have been shaped within this environment. To separate ourselves from this complexity, and to ignore that we are an integral part of it, weakens us as a species in many ways. Physicians above all should recognize that we evolved *with* the apes (as well as the mosquitoes, bacteria, and fungi), and not from them; of course, this is implicit in our use of animal models in medical experiments. As caretakers of our own species, doctors should recognize the ties that bind us to those species that surround us.

Even if one were to take the stance that through our consciousness we are special and apart from nature, there remain ethical and esthetic reasons to preserve other species for our own well-being. It seems impossible to ignore the moral obligation to act as benevolent caretaker to the rest of creation that this discussion of consciousness implies—although most of Judeo-Christian history provides striking examples and justifications to the contrary. But there need be no religious conflict in this matter. It is doubtful that by giving us "dominion over all," God intended us to destroy the other elements of creation. One theologian writes that "to wipe out unnecessarily whole species of those creatures over whom we exercise stewardship is to betray that stewardship and to impoverish the experience of God. It is a crime against our Creator" [11].

Tropical and temperate forests have provided us with some of our most valuable pharmaceuticals in the past.

Humans respond deeply to the esthetics of our environment and its diversity. Ehrlich and Wilson point out the popularity of ecotourism and other activities designed to seek out diversity on the planet. As a species, humans are curious; we search out the unusual and try to understand it. Since the fossil record shows that widespread "weedy" species have been the survivors of past extinctions, our future vacations and scientific forays may remain closer to home—we can find rats, cockroaches, and common weeds in any major city. We also depend upon our diverse environment psychologically, and the retreat to natural surroundings has long been advocated for ailments of both body and spirit. Through experiencing ecological diversity we escape everyday uniformity and feel that we are an integral and connected part of the natural world with a sense of place within our universe. In *A Sand County Almanac*, Aldo Leopold makes a plea to preserve wilderness because it provides "definition and meaning" to life, and for the benefit "of those who may one day wish to see, feel, or study the origins of their cultural inheritance" [12].

Conservationists, such as Aldo Leopold, Henry David Thoreau, or John Muir, often write about the value of wilderness and diversity for its own sake, completely apart from its value for humanity. Unfortunately, the rate of global deforestation does not afford us the time it will take to raise public consciousness to this level of awareness and action. According to James D. Nations, Research Director at the Center for Human Ecology:

> The day may come when ethical considerations about biological diversity become our most important reason for species conservation. But in the meantime, if we want to

hold onto our planet's biological diversity, we have to speak the vernacular. And that vernacular is utility, economics, and the well-being of individual human beings [13].

Medicine and food

In the past decade, there has been a resurgence of interest in exploring tropical rain forests for their medicinal value. As well publicized studies by Norman Farnsworth and others have shown, up to 25% of all prescription drugs contain a plant-derived active ingredient, and there are 18 drugs currently used in the United States that are obtained directly from forest plants [14]. Among the most important of these drugs are vincristine and vinblastine, which are antimitotic alkaloids derived from the rosy periwinkle plant. Vincristine is used as part of the MOPP chemotherapy regimen, and has helped increase the rate of remission in acute childhood leukemia from 20% to 90%. On the international level, quinine, from the bark of the cinchona tree, is another indispensable drug in our pharmacopoeia. It is the treatment of choice for the acute stage of *Plasmodium falciparum* malaria, and has remained effective despite widespread resistance to chloroquine and other synthetic derivatives. Plant-based antioxidants are among the many natural products being screened to fight HIV, and even the inhabitants of the forests are now being studied for their medicinal value; leeches, snakes, ticks, and vampire bats are currently being used to develop new anticoagulants [15].

Tropical and temperate forests have provided us with some of our most valuable pharmaceuticals in the past, and they remain a potential site for new discovery. Most drug development programs turned towards synthetics and molecular modeling beginning in the 1940s, and there is no doubt that biomolecular engineering remains the most valuable tool in current development programs. However, there are both imaginative and scientific limitations to this approach. Natural products, particularly tropical rain forest plants, remain an essential source of bioactive compounds. Following the lead of the National Cancer Institute, many major pharmaceutical companies have recently modernized their natural product screening programs. Merck has signed an agreement with the National Biodiversity Institute in Costa Rica to screen rain forest plants for medicinal value. Shaman Pharmaceuticals, a small company in California, is using the knowledge of people who live within rain forest regions to search for new drugs, and as a consequence has an antiviral agent in development. In fact, there are 107 companies in the United States now doing research on plant-based medicinals, and many more are involved world-wide. One reason for this renewed interest in natural product screening is the rapid destruction of the world's rain forests. Although 65% to 75% of higher plant species are indigenous to rain forests, Cornell biologist Thomas Eisner estimates that less than 2% have been explored for their medicinal potential [16,17]. The present rate of destruction, as well as the loss of local knowledge as indigenous cultures are destroyed, may prevent any meaningful exploration in the future.

Despite our ever-advancing technology, it is impossible to replace the scientific information locked within the DNA of the rain forest since it has evolved over millions of years of complex co-evolution in a highly competitive environment. Whether a product is used directly, a molecule provides a new idea to a biologist, or a new gene is spliced into a strain of *Escherichia coli* makes little difference. We run the risk of burning down this vast library just as we are finding the proper keys to use it. In what he calls "an urgent race against time," Michael Balick of the New York Botanical Garden states: "As tropical forests are destroyed and tribal peoples accultured, our ability to discover new pharmaceutical agents and bring them into everyday use is being seriously compromised" [18].

Crop diversity is also critical for the protection of the world's food supply, and deforestation threatens both the wild relatives of major crops and the supply of alternative foods in times of famine. Fifteen thousand years ago, humans used thousands of kinds of plants as nourishment. With the domestication of crops, this diversity in kinds of plants eaten decreased dramatically, but the diversity within each crop increased as a result of their exposure to new environments and the rise of traditional farming practices. Today, this diversity is threatened. As the result of high-yielding seeds and well-meaning distribution programs, food crop diversity has declined dramatically on the planet. Two decades ago, Garrison Wilkes said:

> Suddenly . . . we are discovering Mexican farmers planting hybrid corn seeds from a midwestern seed firm, Tibetan farmers planting barley from a Scandinavian plant breeding station, and Turkish farmers planting wheat from the Mexican wheat program. Each of these classic areas of crop-specific genetic diversity is rapidly becoming an area of seed uniformity [19].

The global consequences of diversity loss could dwarf the nineteenth century regional example of the Irish potato famine. Then, the reliance on only two strains of potatoes allowed the potato blight *Phytophora infestans* to decimate the potato crop for five years. One to two million people died of starvation and its related diseases, and as many more migrated to North America. Only the discovery of resistant wild strains in the Andes and Mexico has allowed the world's potato crop to thrive today [20]. As crop failure and disease occur, we must often look to the tropics—and often the tropical forests—to cross-breed the genetic information of wild and semidomesticated relatives of commercial species. One species of wild rice from India already serves to protect the crops in Asia from the four major rice diseases, and in Africa and India the introduction of wild Brazilian cassava genes to provide disease resistance has increased the yield of this important food crop by 18-fold [21]. High in the Peruvian Andes tomato seed No. 832 was collected in 1962; when backcrossed 10 generations with a commercial variety, it proceeded to yield a larger tomato with an increased sugar content—a discovery worth about $8 million per year to the tomato industry as of 1986 [22].

In 1981 it was estimated that 80% of the world's food supply was based on fewer than two dozen species [13]. Revised estimates, based on national supply rather than production data, more accurately estimate that 103 species contribute about 90% of the national per capita supplies of food plants [23]. Although this revision should not undermine the important argument for preserving the genetic diversity of the world's major commercial crops, it does serve to introduce a new aspect of the discussion. The conservation of plant species diversity remains important for its direct nutritional value as well as the value of maintaining genetic variants. This nutritional diversity depends largely on tropical forests. In Nigeria, up to 150 species of woody plants are used locally for nutritional purposes, and over 1,500 wild plants from forests are used in the tropics as leafy vegetables [24]. In sub-Saharan Africa, wild plants from the forests are relied on nutritionally in three ways: 1) minor but sustained use for diversity and variety, 2) major use at specific times in the agricultural year such as the months preceding harvest, and 3) major use during times of drought, since forests survive low rainfall when domestic crops do not [25]. According to biologist Laurence Roche, "Scientists, planners, and politicians have not simply grasped the fact that the survival of a number of small-scale peasant farming systems over much of sub-Saharan Africa depends on the continued existence of natural forest vegetation, woodlands and trees" [24].

The move away from traditional agriculture and forestry practices in Africa has had profound effects, and the continent is fast losing the ability to feed itself. It is estimated that in some areas, the shift to mechanized, large scale monocultures has reduced the human carrying capacity of the land from 25 to 40 individuals per square kilometer to fewer than 10 to 20. These trends are at least partly responsible for the massive human migrations away from small villages and for the increasing spiral of debt and food importation [24]. Similar findings in the Brazilian Amazon document the value of traditional systems of food production and their dependence on forest diversity. For example, by preserving forested river margins, the Tukano Indians of the upper Rio Negro Basin maintain the aquatic diversity of their fisheries. Rather than deforesting these areas for agriculture, they derive significant animal protein through this practice; no experiments can demonstrate comparable agricultural potential on these blackwater soils [26].

Ecological services

The ecological services provided by diverse forest ecosystems are essential for human health. In the years to come, climate change, disruption of hydrological cycles, soil degradation, and water availability will mediate many of deforestation's health effects. Deforestation affects global climate by contributing to the greenhouse effect, and it has important local effects as well. Although the rising level of carbon dioxide in the atmosphere is primarily caused by the consumption of fossil fuels in industrialized countries like the United States, the burning of tropical forests contributes up to 25% of CO_2 emissions. Furthermore, a net loss of forest biomass reduces the effect of the "carbon dioxide sink" that is provided by tropical rain forests [27,28]. The average temperature rise of 0.6°C in the last one hundred years is well documented, and a further increase of 2°C to 5°C is predicted for the next 50 to 100 years as carbon dioxide levels double from their pre-industrial levels [29]. This predicted temperature increase would equal the difference in temperature between the last ice age and the present. The question is, therefore—what are the health implications of such a temperature change?

The direct health effects of global warming will range from an increased mortality among the elderly because of heat waves, to likely changes in the vectors of many tropical diseases such as malaria, dengue fever, arbovirus encephalitis, yellow fever, and Rift Valley fever [1,30]. The indirect effects, though, may be even more dramatic. The expected one meter rise in sea level because of thermal expansion and melting ice-caps could reduce coastal land area by 3% and total crop land by one-third, creating up to 50 million environmental refugees in the process. Coastal cities will be jeopardized, and large portions of low-lying countries such as Bangladesh might disappear, leaving displaced populations nowhere to go in areas already stressed by crowding and overpopulation. As the salinity of water tables rises, more and more land will become unfit for agriculture [30].

The global consequences of diversity loss could dwarf the nineteenth century regional example of the Irish potato famine.

Precipitation will increase as the world's climate heats up, but it will change in distribution and there will likely be an intensification of the extremes of the hydrologic cycle. According to a model designed by the National Aeronautics and Space Administration Goddard Institute, the greenhouse effect will lead to greater frequency and intensity of drought and more intense wet and stormy conditions on the planet. The model predicts no regional "winners"; droughts increase in virtually all low- and middle-latitude land areas, and increased rain occurs in the form of high-intensity storms [31].

If these models prove true, the effect of global warming on agriculture will be disastrous. Climate changes will prevent irrigation from providing the crop protection and yield enhancement we depend on today, and it is unlikely that lost crop area will be offset by the creation of new agricultural belts [32]. Physicist John Holdren predicts that a carbon dioxide-induced climatic change could lead to the death of up to a billion people by famine before 2020 [33]. While this value may seem extreme, the severity of recent famines in Ethiopia and Somalia, combined with trends of decreasing per capita food production worldwide (per capita food production dropped 13% between 1984 and 1988 alone), must cause us to take any further climate-induced stresses upon the world's food supply very seriously [34].

Regional climate changes induced by deforestation will also be substantial. Retreating forest cover has been implicated in rainfall decline in India, Peninsular Malaysia, the Ivory Coast, the Philippines, and in the Panama Canal area. In the Amazon, which recycles between 50% and 80% of its water, deforestation threatens to reduce rainfall across the entire Amazon basin and even into the agricultural lands of southern Brazil. In addition, the albedo effect from removal of vegetation could lead to a new self-perpetuating steady state of cooler soil, lower rainfall, and sparser vegetation [35]. A model by the Center for Ocean-Land-Atmosphere Interactions predicts a longer dry season for deforested Amazonia, thus suggesting that complete and rapid destruction of these tropical rain forests could be irreversible [36].

These changes in the hydrological cycle have global health effects. Severe flooding results from the increased runoff and decreased recycling of rainfall following massive deforestation. In India, the area subject to flooding has more than tripled since 1960, and water tables are going down even where rainfall has been ample. Throughout much of the country, however, droughts have also intensified during this time [37]. In 1988, Bangladesh suffered its worst flood on record when two-thirds of the country was underwater for several days. Up to 25 million people were left homeless, and disease lingered in the flood's wake. Many scientists point to the half deforested middle mountain ranges in Nepal and India as the cause, and also note that the "50 year floods" now seem to come every few years [38]. However, Jack Ives, who coordinates the United Nations Mountain Ecology and Sustainable Development Project, disputes this link between flooding and deforestation in the Himalayas. He states that the evidence is inconclusive, and warns of the danger of blaming the subsistence farmers of the Himalayas for the woes of those on the flood plains below [39].

A carbon dioxide–induced climatic change could lead to the death of up to a billion people by famine before 2020.

Deforestation and its associated biodiversity loss also contributes to soil erosion and land degradation throughout the world. Along with overgrazing, over-cultivation, and salinization, deforestation reduces the water-absorbing capacity of the soil and accelerates runoff. In western Africa, Eneas Salati demonstrated that runoff rates recorded from some cultivated and bare soils were 20-fold higher than those from forests [40,41]. Erosion then leads to further decrease in water retention and a decrease in nutrients, land productivity, and the ability for roots to take hold. Rivers, lakes, and reservoirs silt up, leading to decreased storage area and increased flooding [28]. The U.S. Department of Soil and Water Conservation estimates that between 30 and 75 tons of soil are washed away annually from each hectare of deforested land in Nepal [24]. Similarly, in Ethiopia's regions of endemic famine, massive soil erosion has resulted from deforestation of whole mountain catchment areas. Complex nutrient cycles are affected as well, and World Bank ecologist Kenneth Newcombe notes that when land is without trees, mineral nutrients are not recycled from deep soil layers and soil fertility declines [42]. The end result of this erosion and degradation is famine. Lester Brown writes that in Africa, which has the world's fastest population growth rate, "a combination of deforestation, overgrazing, soil erosion, and desertification contributed to a lowering of per capita grain production by some 17% from the historical peak in the late 1960s" [42].

Lastly, the issue of water availability is crucial to human health, and it is affected by each of the previously mentioned changes in climate, hydrological cycles, and soil degradation. The WHO report, *Our Planet, Our*

Health, states that nearly 50% of the world's population suffers from diseases associated with insufficient or contaminated water, and that four million children die of waterborne and foodborne diarrheal diseases each year. Typhoid, cholera, amebic infections, bacillary dysentery, and other diarrheal diseases cause morbidity representing as much as 80% of all sicknesses [1]. The World Commission on Environment and Development states, "In the developing world, the number of water taps nearby is a better indication of the health of a community than the number of hospital beds" [7]. Norman Myers, in his book *Primary Source,* notes that tropical forests make a substantial contribution to public health by assuring dependable supplies of good-quality drinking water. In many deforested regions, the quality of drinking water has dropped as sources shift from fresh forest streams toward contaminated rivers or ponds [28]. Decline in the quantity and quality of water supplies because of deforestation has set back public health programs in major cities such as Bangkok and Manila. In Malaysia, the price of water from a catchment with undisturbed forest increases twofold after the forest is subject to controlled logging, and fourfold when uncontrolled logging is allowed [43].

Ehrlich and Wilson point out that there is no way to replace the various ecological services provided by natural ecosystems. Virtually all attempts at large-scale inorganic substitution have failed: synthetic pesticides, inorganic fertilizer, chlorination of water for purification, dams for flood and drought protection, and even air-conditioning cannot measure up against natural counterparts provided by forest cover and ecosystem diversity. In addition to short-term problems, these measures generally require large energy subsidies, and thus add to our long-term environmental impact as well [10].

Perhaps the best summary of the ecological impact of deforestation comes from a French forester in Africa more than 50 years ago. In *The Disappearance of the Tropical Forests of Africa,* A.M.A. Aubreville writes prophetically:

> We are witnessing the death struggle of a plant world, slow stages in the drying up and degeneration of tropical Africa . . . it is probable that the wholesale destruction of inland forests will accelerate deterioration of vegetation and soil in Africa and bring acute desert conditions. . . . The insidious thing about it is that, generally speaking, nobody seems to realize it. In much the same way that the friends of a sick man, who has been an invalid for years, get used to seeing him in an ailing condition that they forget he was once in perfect health. They cease to perceive the slow encroachment of the disease until one day the sick man dies [44].

Direct health effects

The health effects directly associated with deforestation have received little attention from either environmentalists or the medical community. This is understandable, given the difficult task of raising public awareness about even the most global issues such as climate change or species loss. However, diseases caused by tropical deforestation can undermine development schemes, and, when combined with associated health problems from urbanization and poverty, have a significant impact upon the world's health. Malaria is currently the most important disease associated with deforestation, particularly in the Amazon.

Malaria spreads at the forest fringes, and deforestation has increased transmission in tropical areas ranging from Southeast Asia to the Amazon. *Anopheles dirus,* one vector of the most deadly type of malaria, *Plasmodium falciparum,* has been shown to breed in pools around partly cleared forests [1]. New roads into the Amazon have likewise created ideal habitats along their flooded embankments for the *Anopheles darlingi* mosquito, which is the most important malaria vector in the region. Soil erosion from farming and mining also creates breeding sites around the forest [45]. One study of hospital records from three rural areas of the Amazon basin reveals that the number of cases of malaria increased fivefold from 1983 to 1987; that the predominant parasite changed from *Plasmodium vivax* to *Plasmodium falciparum;* and that increased malaria followed increased immigration and colonization of the forest. This same epidemiological data showed malaria rates of 1% to 2% in the most stable community, 8% to 9% in a growing community, and 14% to 26% in the new forest settlements [46].

Deforestation has increased [malaria] transmission in tropical areas ranging from Southeast Asia to the Amazon.

Regional data support these local observations. In 1983 there were 287,000 cases of malaria in the Brazilian Amazon, and this figure rose to 500,000 by 1988. Aside from the massive migration of settlers into the region and the creation of new breeding sites for mosquitoes, there are new problems facing public health officials battling this epidemic. Spraying dwellings is no longer an effective control measure, since for unknown reasons the Amazonian variety of *Anopheles darlingi* prefers the outdoors between feedings. New World Bank loans include money for indoor spraying with DDT and other insecticides to control the problem, but evaluating the impact of this strategy will prove difficult since little is known about the habits of forest mosquitoes [45].

In his book *Rainforest Corridors,* Nigel J.H. Smith demonstrates that in addition to the current malaria problem, deforestation and settlement of the Amazon pose a number of potential public health risks [47]. Onchocerciasis was first documented in Brazil in the 1970s, and if it were to take root in the Amazon it could become a major health concern; in parts of Africa, it has forced people to abandon villages and cultivated land. The vector for Bancroft's filariasis thrives along the Transamazon Highway, and the disease threatens to become more significant as population in the region increases. Schistosomiasis has occurred in isolated areas of the Amazon, but could easily spread as humans alter ecosystems (as happened in Africa following hydroelectric and irrigation projects) and as both infected individuals and appropriate vectors are introduced along the Transamazon. New settlement and new highways will likely increase the transmission of Chagas' disease; vectors already exist, and the spraying programs designed to control malaria may aid their further spread by wiping out natural predators in the rain forest. Finally, the conditions along the Transamazon are appropriate for an epidemic of yellow fever, and this disease could present yet another public health problem as settlement increases.

Another example of deforestation's direct health effects is the increasing number of landslides in deforested hills.

The existing malaria epidemic in the Amazon raises the issue of how little attention has been paid to the impact of development on public health. The World Bank acknowledges that nobody understood the intricate factors contributing to the malaria epidemic in the Amazon until it was already well-established. However, they maintain that the control of adverse health effects from development projects is up to the particular country concerned [45]. Environmentalists disagree and hold the World Bank directly responsible for disasters such as the malaria epidemic. One senior attorney with the Environmental Defense Fund says of a $99 million World Bank loan to control the epidemic, "For a country like Brazil, that's a very expensive way of standing still" [45].

Along with the spread of disease vectors, there are other ways in which deforestation has direct impact upon human health. Lack of firewood creates significant public health problems, particularly in the rural Himalayas and the African Sahel. In the Himalayan foothills, forests have been pushed so far back that women now spend an additional 1.4 hours per day to collect firewood than they did just 10 years ago. This is time spent away from the farm, and there has indeed been a concurrent decline in agricultural production by 24% and a decrease in per capita food consumption by an average of 100 calories per day in these areas [43]. Boiling water has become a luxury in many parts of the world, and quick-cooking cereals have replaced more nutritious, slower-cooking foods such as beans. As dried dung is used as fuel for cooking rather than fertilizer for the fields, soil fertility suffers; this diversion has been blamed for a 15% decrease in Nepal's crop yield [41].

Another example of deforestation's direct health effects is the increasing number of landslides in deforested hills surrounding many large cities. More than 500 died in one slide in Colombia in 1987, and in 1989 landslides left over 18,000 homeless on the outskirts of Rio de Janeiro and 70,000 homeless in Thailand [38]. Illegal logging was blamed for the flash floods and mudslides that killed 6,000 people following typhoon Thelma in the Philippines in 1991 [48]. In all of the above cases, deforestation combined with both natural forces and urbanization with devastating results.

Urbanization and poverty

One hundred years ago the Earth's urban population was 200 million; by 1990 it had reached two billion. The growth of urban areas by migration from the countryside, particularly in poor and developing countries, is in part related to deforestation. Land degradation—which we have seen is tightly linked to deforestation—has been the major factor in this movement of subsistence farmers into the shantytowns of major cities. This is especially true in the African Sahel, where thousands of villages have been abandoned in recent years. According to Lester Brown, "The drying out and desertification of the Sahelian region probably account for the largest source of environmental refugees in the world today" [42]. The situation is similar in southern Africa, where deforestation accompanied by soil erosion and the depletion of water supplies have forced tens of thousands from their farms and into towns, cities, or relief camps [38].

As yet, there has been little study of the many known and potential health problems associated with such migrations. Transmission of disease may occur either from those who are migrating (active transmitters), or to those who are migrating (passive aquirers). Overall, the trend in Africa has been an increase in "urban" diseases such as TB, water-borne enteric illnesses, and other diseases associated with malnutrition—although cause or effect in urbanization's relationship to disease often remains unclear [49]. As urban growth without improved urban services has occurred, water shortages and problems of waste and sewage disposal have resulted. Paul Epstein points out the link between cholera outbreaks in South America and recent urbanization (Lima's shantytowns, for example) [50]. The World Health Organization warns of future health problems as new roads, reservoirs, drains, land clearance, and deforestation lead to changes in local ecology. They believe that natural foci for disease vectors may be incorporated into the urban sprawl, creating new ecological niches for zoonotic animal reservoirs. Even without appropriate vectors, human migration from rural areas to the Federal District of Brazil has made Chagas' disease one of the leading causes of death in that region [1]. Lastly, a word about AIDS—not its future, but its past. Evolutionary biologist Jared Diamond has presented three theories to explain why AIDS emerged in Africa only recently; one of these speculates that conditions for efficient spread between populations have occurred only in modern times, with the rise of cities, prostitution, venereal diseases, use and reuse of hypodermic syringes for medical care, and movements of people over long distances [51].

Toward a sustainable future

Deforestation illustrates the connection between environmental problems and human health. The effects of global forest losses are far-reaching; biodiversity loss threatens our ethical and esthetic senses, our supply of medicine and food, and the ecological interactions we depend on to regulate our environment. Deforestation also has direct health effects, by, for example, altering disease vectors and increasing the vulnerability of marginal populations to disasters such as landslides and floods. Deforestation also helps drive the downward spiral of migration, urbanization, and poverty.

Environmental stresses are closely linked with each other, with patterns of economic development, and with social and political factors; all of these issues affect human health. Looming in the background is overpopulation. By the year 2020 the United Nations predicts a world population of eight billion [1], and any environmental or health program must account for this exponential growth. The downward spiral of poverty and environmental destruction is fueled by population pressures, and to break this cycle these pressures must be controlled. The World Health Organization advocates the same steps to reduce both infant mortality and to decrease fertility—improved maternal health and education; improved water supply, sanitation and nutrition; and family planning integrated with health care programs [1]. Others feel this argument is flawed and advocate more stringent measures following the Chinese model of strict birth control [52]. In either case, population control must play a central role in any sustainable public health policy.

Forest products can be renewably extracted such that the forest is worth more standing than cut.

"Sustainability," as applied to the discussion of rain forests, implies attractive alternatives to the problem of short-term destruction for lumber and agriculture: forest products can be renewably extracted such that the forest is worth more standing than cut, and local economies are bolstered in the process. Biodiversity can also be preserved and studied, with the economic gains from discoveries partially returned to local economies. However, when the word "sustainability" is applied to public health, it is more troublesome: Should all practical public health interventions, designed to sustain human life, be pursued regardless of their long-term demographic consequences? Is there a danger of increasing population and environmental pressures through these interventions, and if so can we justify inaction under some circumstances? These are complicated questions, and at their heart lie conflicting ethical premises and policy missions. Ecological approaches imply giving priority to populations, not individuals. As hard choices are forced upon us in the future, we must search for an inclusive definition of sustainability through the integration of economic, environmental, population, and public health policies.

We are now standing at a crossroad. We know enough about the earth's environmental problems to be concerned for our future, but we debate how much action is justified and remain unsure how to prioritize these actions. In *The Youngest Science*, Lewis Thomas examines our limitations:

> We do not know enough about ourselves. We are ignorant about how we work, about how we fit in, and most of all about the enormous, imponderable system of life in which we are imbedded as working parts. We do not really understand nature, at all. We have come a long way, indeed, but just enough to become conscious of our own ignorance. . . .
> It is a new experience for all of us [53].

Admitting ignorance yet struggling against it is a difficult task, but important. We must learn to become comfortable as working parts in nature's imponderable system, even as we endeavor to manage it wisely.

Notes

1. World Health Organization Commission of Health and Environment. Our planet, our health. Geneva: World Health Organization, 1992.

2. World Development Report 1992. World development indicators. New York: Oxford University Press, 1992:1–24.

3. Wilson EO. The diversity of life. Cambridge: Harvard University Press, 1992.

4. Durning AB. Ending poverty. In: Brown LR, ed. State of the world 1990. New York: W.W. Norton and Company, 1990:138.

5. Chowdhry K. Poverty, environment, development. Daedalus 1989; 118:141–157.

6. Wilson EO. The current state of biological diversity. In: Wilson EO, ed. Biodiversity. Washington, DC: National Academy Press, 1988:5.

7. World Commission on Environment and Development. Our common future. New York: Oxford University Press, 1987.

8. Lugo A. Estimating the reductions in the biodiversity of tropical forest species. In: Wilson EO, ed. Biodiversity. Washington, DC: National Academy Press, 1988:63–67.

9. Stevens WK. Species loss: crisis or false alarm. The New York Times, August 20, 1991; B5.

10. Ehrlich PR, Wilson EO. Biodiversity studies: science and policy. Science 1991; 253:758–762.

11. Cobb JB Jr. A Christian view of biodiversity. In: Wilson EO, ed. Biodiversity. Washington, DC: National Academy Press, 1988:485.

12. Leopold A. A Sand County almanac. New York: Oxford University Press, 1949.

13. Nations JD. Deep ecology meets the developing world. In: Wilson EO, ed. Biodiversity. Washington, DC: National Academy Press, 1988:81.

14. Farnsworth NR. The role of ethnopharmacology in drug development. In: Chadwick DJ, ed. Bioactive compounds from plants. New York: John Wiley and Sons, 1990:2–11.

15. Bang NU. Leeches, snakes, ticks, and vampire bats in today's cardiovascular drug development. Circulation 1991;84:436.

16. Principe PP. Medicinal plants: values and development options. Presented at Investment Priorities for Biodiversity Conservation in the Asia/Pacific Region Group; June 22, 1990; Washington, DC.

17. Eisner T. Cited in: Joyce C. Prospectors for tropical medicines. New Scientist 1991;19:38.

18. Balick MJ. Ethnobotany and the identification of therapeutic agents from plants. In: Chadwick DJ, ed. Bioactive compounds from plants. New York: John Wiley and Sons, 1990:22–31.

19. Wilkes G. As quoted in: Fowler C, Mooney P. Shattering. Tucson: The University of Arizona Press, 1990.

20. Fowler C, Mooney P. Shattering. Tucson: The University of Arizona Press, 1990.

21. Plotkin MJ. The outlook for new agricultural and industrial products from the tropics. In: Wilson EO, ed. Biodiversity. Washington, DC: National Academy Press, 1988:110.

22. Iltus HH. Serendipity in the exploration of biodiversity. In: Wilson EO, ed. Biodiversity. Washington, DC: National Academy Press, 1988:101–103.

23. Prescott-Allen R, Prescott-Allen C. How many plants feed the world? Conservation Biology 1990;4:365–374.

24. Roche L. Forestry and famine: arguments against growth without development. Ecologist 1989;19:16–21.

25. Grivetti LE. Bush foods and edible weeds of agriculture. In: Akhtar R, ed. Health and disease in tropical Africa: geographical and medical viewpoints. New York: Harwood Academic Publications, 1987:68.

26. Chernela JM. Managing rivers of hunger: the Tukano of Brazil. Advances in Economic Botany 1989;7:238–248.

27. Salati E. Deforestation and its role in possible changes in the Brazilian Amazon. In: DeFries RS, ed. Global change and our common future. Washington: National Academy Press, 1989:159–171.

28. Myers N. The primary source. New York: W.W. Norton and Company, 1984.

29. Leaf A. Potential health effects of global climatic and environmental changes. N Eng J Med 1989;321:1577–1583.

30. Godlee F. Health implications of climatic change. BMJ 1991;303: 1254–1256.

31. Hansen J. Regional greenhouse climate effects. In: Proceedings of Second North American Conference on Preparing for Climate Change. Washington, DC: Government Institute, Inc., 1989.

32. Ehrlich PR, Daily GC, Ehrlich AH. Global change and carrying capacity: implications for life on earth. In: DeFries RS, ed. Global change and our common future. Washington, DC: National Academy Press, 1989:19–30.

33. Holdren J. Cited in: Ehrlich P. The loss of diversity. In: Wilson EO, ed. Biodiversity. Washington, DC: National Academy Press, 1988:24.

34. Bello M. Deteriorating environment highlight of conference. National Research Council News Report, June 1989.

35. Myers N. Tropical deforestation and climatic change. Environmental Conservation 1988;15:293–297.

36. Shulka J. Amazon deforestation and climate change. Science 1990; 247:1322–1325.

37. Brown LR, Young JE. Feeding the world in the nineties. In: Brown LR, ed. State of the world 1990. New York: W.W. Norton and Company, 1990:61.

38. Jacobson JL. Abandoning homelands. In: Brown LR, ed. State of the world 1989. New York: W.W. Norton and Company, 1989:65.

39. Ives J. Floods in Bangladesh: who is to blame? New Scientist 1991; 130:34–37.

40. Postel S. Halting land degradation. In: Brown LR, ed. State of the world 1989. New York: W.W. Norton and Company, 1989:26.

41. Salati E. Cited in: Postel S. Reforesting the earth. In: Brown LR, ed. State of the world 1988. New York: W.W. Norton and Company, 1988:91.

42. Newcombe K. Cited in: Brown LR. What does global change mean for society? In: DeFries RS, ed. Global change and our common future. Washington, DC: National Academy Press, 1989:103–124.

43. Mellor JW. The intertwining of governmental problems and poverty. Environment 1988;30:8–16.

44. Aubreville AMA. Cited in: Roche L. Forestry and famine: arguments against growth without development. Ecologist 1989:16.

45. Kingman S. Malaria runs riot on Brazil's wild frontier. New Scientist 1989; 123:24–25.

46. McGreevy PB. Effects of immigration on the prevalence of malaria in rural areas of the Amazon basin. Memorias Do Instituto Oswaldo Cruz, 1989;84:485–491.

47. Smith NJH. Rainforest corridors: the transamazon colonization scheme. Berkeley: University of California Press, 1982.

48. Hunt P. Loggers blamed for typhoon deaths. New Scientist 1991;132:14.

49. Prothero RM. Population movements and health hazards in tropical Africa. In: Akhtar R, ed. Health and disease in tropical Africa: geographical and medical viewpoints. New York: Harwood Academic Publications, 1987:84.

50. Epstein PR. Cholera and the environment: an introduction to climate change. PSR Quarterly 1992;2:146–160.

51. Diamond J. The mysterious origins of AIDS. Natural History, September 1992;24–29.

52. King M. Public health and the ethics of sustainability. Trop Geogr Med 1990;42:199.

53. Thomas L. The youngest science: notes of a medicine watcher. New York: Bantam Books, 1984.

6

Hardwood Logging Does Not Harm Tropical Rainforests

International Wood Products Association

The International Wood Products Association (IHPA) is an Alexandria, Virginia, organization that represents U.S. importers of wood and wood products and that encourages forest conservation and reforestation.

The logging of tropical forests by producers of hardwood products is not the main cause of tropical deforestation. The primary causes of deforestation are the clearing of land for agriculture and the use of trees for fuelwood. The harvesting of hardwood trees need not be harmful. Forestry practices that encourage the continued growth of hardwood trees can both protect rainforests and generate income for people in timber-producing areas.

Why do we use wood?
    Wood has a wide variety of uses. It's used in construction, furniture, paper, toys, flooring, boats, musical instruments and much more. Trees are renewable; you can grow new ones by planting seeds. Wood is natural. It's organic, nontoxic, recyclable, and biodegradable. Wood helps to conserve energy; turning a tree into sawn wood or veneer requires less energy and heat, and creates less pollution, than processing other materials that serve similar purposes.
    What are rainforests and where are they located?
    Rainforests are thick, wet forests that have an average annual rainfall of more than four feet, a rich diversity of species, and extremely high volumes of vegetation per unit area. In the tropics, rainforests account for about two-thirds of the forests and are clustered around the equator, primarily in developing countries with few resources and growing populations. Tropical seasonal forests, on the other hand, have more distinct wet and dry phases. Located on the fringes of the rainforests, their structure is simpler, having lower canopies and a more homogenous species mix. Though both have valuable timber resources, the seasonal forests have

From "Some Frequently Asked Questions About Forests," in the International Wood Products Association's (IHPA's) C.U.R.E. Program *Resource Guide*, April 1995. Reprinted by permission of IHPA.

supplied the majority of timber coming from these areas. Rainforests also exist in other climates outside of the tropics—even in Alaska.

What's different about wood from the tropical rainforests?

Tropical hardwoods have unique properties not found in other wood species. Tropical hardwoods grow very slowly and, as a result, many of these species are very strong and extremely weather-resistant. Teak, for example, is associated with sailboats because of its virtual imperviousness to water and weather. Tropical hardwoods don't need to be treated chemically as other woods do for outside, weight-supporting uses. That's why outdoor furniture is often made of these materials. The "boardwalks" in many of our coastal cities are often made of one of these woods. Also, because of their unique characteristics, tropical woods are often used for furniture, cabinets, and wall paneling.

It is important to realize the contribution of forestry to the national economy of developing countries.

How does buying wood products help to save the forests?

The overwhelming reason for the loss of trees (deforestation) in tropical, developing countries is the clearing of land for agricultural/grazing purposes, and the cutting of trees for fuelwood for domestic or industrial use. In these developing countries, deforestation cannot be isolated from social and economic issues such as rapidly expanding populations and extreme poverty. If land has more value when used for subsistence farming or cattle grazing, the forests will be cut down to permit these alternative practices. Trees must be given economic value if they are to be deemed worth saving by the people living in tropical countries. More and more, they are learning that it is important to care for growing trees, and to plant more. Every year, they can cut some trees and sell them for money to meet their current needs. And, if the trees are cut and removed carefully, the smaller trees will continue to grow strong and can be removed later. In this way, these people can make money by carefully growing and harvesting trees, instead of clearing them away to plant crops or graze cattle.

It is important to realize the contribution of forestry to the national economy of developing countries and to the development of rural communities. Since many people in these tropical, timber-producing countries depend on forest industries for their jobs, total preservation of tropical forests is bound to fail. But, conservation and utilization can go hand-in-hand, if done carefully, wisely.

What are some of the ways trees are removed from forests?

Every day, people are learning more about removing some trees carefully, while being sure those left behind are not damaged and that new trees can grow. This is one aspect of forest management. Different types of forests require different types of management. Different logging systems are used to achieve different goals. Usually what loggers want to do is to try to mimic, as much as possible, the forest's natural disturbance regime—that is, nature's own selection process.

For example, in the western U.S., fires are the natural disturbance regime and often level most of the forest. Here, a clear cut is not necessarily inappropriate. In the tropical rainforest, however, massive fires don't occur, so clear cutting does not make sense and is not practiced there. What occurs in the tropics are natural blowdowns or natural die-offs of trees, which leave smaller gaps in the forests than fires do. Commercial logging in the tropics is usually conducted on a "selective" basis so that only a certain number of desirable species of marketable size are cut. Others are left to continue to grow for future use. Some logging operations are very modern and use machinery to remove logs. Helicopters are used in some areas. Other operations are very traditional and use oxen, or even manpower, to move the logs.

Limited endangerment

I've heard that many of these trees are endangered species. How can I find out which are, and which aren't?

Only a couple of tree species have been found to be "endangered" after a thorough study of the scientific data. There is one international organization, the Convention on International Trade in Endangered Species, also known as CITES, that considers the scientific information available about a species, and determines whether or not it is "endangered" or even "threatened." This is the "official" international "endangered species list" and its findings have the power of international law. Almost 130 countries have signed this agreement. This is the group that is credited with saving the elephant, some whale species, and other animals and plants in danger.

CITES Appendix I contains those species found to be "endangered." The only timber species on this list are Alerce, primarily from Chile, in South America, and Brazilian Rosewood. International trade of products of these species is banned, although transactions involving stocks obtained before the listing are allowed, with the proper permits.

CITES Appendix II contains "threatened" species. Trade in products of these species is allowed only after the proper authorities have determined that obtaining that individual shipment did not constitute a threat to the health of that species. The required export permit certifies that certain environmental standards and safeguards were met in order to allow continued trade. The primary timber species on Appendix II are Afrormosia, from Africa, Cuban Mahogany and Mexican Mahogany. The mahogany you see in furniture and other products is almost exclusively Brazilian Mahogany, which is not on either of the lists.

There are many examples of replanting and other reforestation programs around the world.

So, if something is truly "endangered," you probably couldn't get it if you wanted to. And, what is available of species that may be "threatened" has already passed certain environmental tests in order just to be available. CITES lists are available from the U.S. Fish and Wildlife Service, the Tropical Forest Foundation, or the International Wood Products Association.

Is anyone replanting trees?

Yes. There are many examples of replanting and other reforestation programs around the world. Most major forested countries have developed and implemented reforestation programs that replenish and supplement timber growth in existing forest areas. Tree "plantations" are another way to practice replanting. These plantations grow and harvest fuelwood and pulpwood, usually from fast-growing species that produce high volumes relatively quickly (usually 5–10 years vs. the 40 or more required for a hardwood timber tree to reach harvesting size). They are often located in cut-over and non-productive land areas. Successful reforestation occurs through a strong commitment of local and national governments and private forest products companies.

Additionally, there are numerous government aid programs and private programs, like IHPA's "Johnny Mahoganyseed," that are aimed at replanting and at reclaiming abandoned agricultural and degraded forest area. It should also be noted that natural forests have the ability to regenerate themselves. If harvesting operations are carefully and thoughtfully carried out, natural regeneration may be sufficient to sustain the forest.

The [wood products] industry will survive only if it works to ensure the future of our forest resources and the diversity of life they contain.

Are there any hardwood plantations?

Numerous tropical hardwood species have been grown successfully on "plantations." Although there are often serious problems that must be overcome (primarily insect pest problems), a significant amount of wood is produced from these operations. For instance, in the 1800's the British began teak plantations (primarily for military and commercial shipbuilding) in many tropical areas that they had colonized. These plantations continue in Central and South America, Africa, and Southeast Asia. A significant amount of the teak imported to the U.S. comes from plantations in Honduras and Costa Rica. The fifth and sixth leading producing areas for mahogany imports to the U.S. are plantations in Indonesia and Malaysia.

Who protects trees in the U.S.? And what about other countries?

In the United States, unlike in most developing countries, the majority of forested land is privately owned and managed. In most of these areas, and particularly in those areas managed for timber, three-quarters of a billion trees are planted annually by the companies that manage them. The U.S. Forest Service is responsible for protecting the national forests and other federally owned land. They either directly manage or supervise companies they allow on these lands. Other countries usually have an equivalent government agency. Many employ what is known as a "concession" system where a company is granted the right to manage a certain tract of land for a specified amount of time. In other countries, companies buy the forest from the government and it becomes private. Most of these countries, regardless of the particular system they utilize, have national forestry laws and management plans to which everyone must adhere.

Aren't we running out of trees?

No. In some areas there are actually more trees than in the recent past.

For example, in the northeastern U.S. the answer is absolutely not. There are more trees today than there were 100 years ago. In the tropics, however, the actual number of trees has been decreasing, primarily due to clearing of forests for alternative land uses like agriculture. Rates of deforestation have been slowing in these countries in recent years, however, primarily due to improved government policies and enforcement and improved management. Most of these countries also are setting aside vast tracts of forested areas and creating parks and reserves that will never be developed.

Why does the timber industry care about saving the forests?

Besides being the right thing to do, the wood products industry wants an on-going source of supply. The industry will survive only if it works to ensure the future of our forest resources and the diversity of life they contain. Quite simply, no trees = no wood = no industry. Additionally, if trees get scarce, the price of wood products would rise to the point where consumers would look at lesser-desired, but cheaper, substitute materials. So, it is in the best interest of the industry to have an abundance of trees. But, everyone has a reason to work for this cause since forests are so important to the climatic and biological health of our planet.

How many people are employed by the timber industry? What are its revenues?

In the U.S., it is estimated that approximately a million and a half people earn their livings from the forest products industry. Around the world, tens of millions of people are directly employed, and tens of millions more indirectly depend on this industry.

The forest products industry is among the top revenue producers for a number of developing countries. For instance, it is second only to oil and gas in Indonesia and the second largest employer and contributor to GNP [gross national product] in Gabon.

U.S. imports

Does bringing wood into the U.S. from other countries destroy tropical rainforests?

No. As a matter of fact, when we buy these products from developing countries, we are actually helping to save the forests by providing an economic reason to carefully manage them. If we would stop buying these products, we would remove the incentive to manage the forests and we would actually encourage their conversion to other uses, which is exactly what we're trying to avoid.

Let's determine the extent of U.S. responsibility for tropical forest *depletion* by doing a few quick calculations. (*Deforestation* is the complete removal of trees. The role of the forest products industry in this is insignificant. *Depletion* is a loss of biomass that results from the removal of any trees.)

- According to a study commissioned by Greenpeace in Germany, and conducted by a reputable German organization, "forestry" is responsible for an average of about six percent (.06) of forest depletion in tropical countries. (Though we don't know exactly what their term "forestry" includes, we must assume it covers all forestry activities, including fuelwood gathering, etc. This number is "in-the-same-ballpark" with those contained in a similar study conducted by the London Environmental Economics Centre.

- Only about 17% (.17) of all tropical roundwood production is used for "industrial purposes." The remaining is used for fuelwood and other non-industrial purposes. Of the industrial wood and wood products (logs, sawnwood, veneer and plywood) produced in tropical countries, approximately 81.5% (.815) is consumed in those countries. This means that only about 18.5% (.185) goes into the international market. And that even if you totally shut down the entire international trade in tropical woods, you would still have approximately 98.9% of the problem left to address!
- U.S. imports of tropical wood and wood products in 1993 made up approximately 4% (.04) of the total tropical timber market. Japan was, by far, the leading market (approx. 40%), followed by the E.U. [European Union] (19.5%), Taiwan (13%), Korea (13%), and the People's Republic of China (11%).

To determine the role of U.S. wood and wood product imports in tropical forest depletion, multiply the .06 (1) $\times$ .17 (2) $\times$ .185 (2) $\times$ .04 (3). The resulting number, .0000754 (or approximately seven and a half one-thousandths of one percent), is the level of responsibility of the U.S. tropical timber trade.

As you can see, the wood products industry is a very, very small part of the problem of losing trees in the tropical forests, but can be a very large part of the solution.

American consumers should not avoid, or feel bad about buying tropical wood products. On the contrary, a significant proportion of the hundreds of millions of dollars these imports represent (on top of the billions of dollars the Japanese and E.U. markets represent) make their way back to the forests and provide some resources to address the real problems facing the forests: poverty and population pressures.

Management of tropical forests for commercial purposes is more likely to protect them from disappearing than are other uses of the land.

How do we know when we are buying something that it didn't come from improperly managed forests?

Unfortunately, it is extremely difficult to trace the exact source of tropical woods and to further determine how the particular forest, from which that wood originated, is managed. Until adequate information on sustainable forest management is more widely available, consumers should try to learn as much as possible about the source of tropical woods in general. The Tropical Forest Foundation (TFF) is a good source of information. TFF gathers and provides information on tropical forest use and management and has compiled a list of questions designed to help consumers gather information. Additionally, IHPA–The International Wood Products Association has developed for the use of its members environmental and purchasing policies that actively seek information regarding the sources of their supplies and recognize those suppliers who are 1) adhering to all forestry laws of the country concerned, and 2) utilizing good silvicultural and logging practices. Consumers should ensure that the product they are contemplating purchasing was obtained through a current IHPA member.

What is illegal logging?

Illegal logging means breaking laws and regulations associated with harvesting activities, such as logging protected species, logging in protected areas, logging outside of concession boundaries, logging in environmentally sensitive areas, removing under-sized or over-sized trees, extracting more than the allowable harvest, or just logging without authorization or permit. These activities may be carried out by unscrupulous commercial operators or by individual small farmers to obtain firewood or to clear land for agriculture.

Tree plantations . . . are only one form of sustained-yield forestry.

Many tropical countries do not have fully developed land-tenure systems currently set up and operating. Many have enacted new laws or changed old ones recently to reflect increased concerns regarding the forests and indigenous peoples. Many of these laws are written in a way that causes wide variations in interpretation. These continuous changes and the resulting confusion have resulted in a sometimes large "gray area" regarding what is "legal" and what is not "legal." Accusations have been made, and many of these questions are being addressed by courts and legislatures. Let's remember that the accused are innocent until proven guilty and let's all hope that these issues get resolved as soon as possible.

Why aren't bans and boycotts good solutions to the problems in the rainforests?

Timber harvesting is not the primary cause of deforestation, and most of the timber extracted from tropical forests is not exported. Bans and boycotts serve no constructive purpose in encouraging tropical countries to conserve and properly manage their forests. In the tropics, as elsewhere, forestry must compete with alternative forms of land use. Timber boycotts tend to depress the value of tropical hardwoods and the forests that contain them, thus diminishing the incentives to conserve and manage the forests in the face of competing, more destructive land uses. Management of tropical forests for commercial purposes is more likely to protect them from disappearing than are other uses of the land. Additionally, the proceeds from sales of tropical forest products provide resources to address the real problems in these areas.

Are indigenous people in tropical countries being exploited?

There have been some news stories reporting that a few indigenous tribes in a couple of tropical countries have been exploited by unscrupulous entrepreneurs. One cannot dispute that low standards of living make exploitation possible. The answer is for industry and local and national governments in developing countries to work together to help indigenous populations develop economically while protecting to the greatest extent possible both the environment and their cultural values.

If the goal is to help indigenous cultures develop economies to improve their standard of living, why not fund less destructive ways of using the forests, such as harvesting nuts, rubber and other natural products?

All practices that give value to the forests are worth exploring and developing. However, harvesting nuts and rubber applies to fewer species of trees and gives less value to trees than does timber harvesting.

Are there any countries where rainforest loss has been slowed or halted?

Yes. Many tropical countries are making strides in slowing deforestation. For instance, from 1992 to 1995 the rate of deforestation in Brazil shrank dramatically. This is attributed in no small part to the government's decision to halt the subsidies for clearing land for non-forest uses. Similar successes have been registered elsewhere.

Many of these countries have set aside vast areas for parks, nature reserves, and other uses that will ensure their futures as forest lands. Laws have been passed, and policies developed and implemented, that are very specific as to where certain activities are, and are not, allowed. Violations can result in severe penalties. Fines, and even prison sentences, have already been imposed in some instances. These measures, and others like them, are helping to slow deforestation.

What is the connection between forests and the ozone layer? What about "global warming"?

There is no connection to the ozone layer. The main threat to the ozone layer is from chlorofluorocarbons (CFCs), which are man-made chemicals that largely have been banned from use. Trees have no effect in either producing or mitigating CFCs.

However, forests are an important element in regulating global climate—not only temperature but exchanges of gases in the atmosphere. There is a growing concern that a buildup of carbon dioxide, a harmless atmospheric gas, will cause global warming. Through the process of photosynthesis, trees absorb carbon dioxide and produce oxygen, and thus reduce the potential for global warming. This makes it all the more important that we ensure that we have forests forever.

Organizational help

Are there reputable organizations that are doing positive things to protect the forests?

Yes, many. For example:

- The United Nations established the International Tropical Timber Organization (ITTO), which assists tropical/developing countries in more efficiently managing their resources and industrialized/consuming countries in better utilizing timber products. The ITTO has financed over two hundred projects worth over US $100 million.
- The World Bank is assisting developing nations in monitoring the careful development of their natural resources by funding remote sensing satellites. These satellites are able to see through thick cloud cover which would normally hinder aerial photographers.
- The Tropical Forest Foundation is an educational organization formed by leaders from industry and the scientific and conservation communities. TFF collects and distributes scientific data and other information about sustainable forestry in the world's tropical forests. It also holds educational forums on tropical forest issues

and policies, and has set up low-impact logging and forest-management programs in several tropical areas.

- The U.S. Agency for International Development (AID) is a federal government agency that provides research, training, and economic benefits to developing countries. It has programs that assist in areas such as new management techniques, new harvesting and/or processing technologies, and reforestation/replanting.
- The Food and Agriculture Organization (FAO) of the United Nations is active in a number of programs designed to help countries manage the delicate balance between meeting community needs and preventing deforestation.
- The International Forestry Division of the U.S. Forest Service works closely with AID, and other U.S. government agencies, on programs and policies affecting forest resources around the world. It provides technical expertise and policy analysis, and works on the determination of criteria and indicators for sustainable forest management.

And, there are foreign aid agencies in many industrialized countries that assist developing countries with forestry projects. For instance, the Overseas Development Administration, in the United Kingdom, has an "Approved Forestry Projects" list that contains 185 projects with financing to the tune of approximately US $222 million.

Doesn't sustained yield forestry mean replacing the natural complexity of the rainforest with monoculture and destroying the habitat of many animals?

Not at all, although any human activity in a forest is going to cause some change. There are different ways of practicing good forestry. Tree plantations, which produce one type of tree, are only one form of sustained-yield forestry, and they are often sited in areas where the land has been cut-over or is non-productive. We can also practice sustainable forestry in a way that doesn't destroy the complexity of natural forests—through selective cutting, for example. We may change the composition of the particular stand of trees that we are managing, but we are not necessarily going to lose the different species from it.

What is IHPA and its role in protecting the forests?

IHPA–The International Wood Products Association was founded in 1956 in the United States. IHPA represents U.S. importers of all types of wood and wood products from all over the world. Many companies and trade organizations that are associated with these activities are also members. Over twenty different countries, from all geographic regions of the world, are represented on IHPA's membership rolls.

IHPA has developed and promulgated responsible environmental and purchasing policies for its members. IHPA and its members work to encourage policies in tropical countries to strengthen and enforce forest conservation and reforestation. In 1988, IHPA established the C.U.R.E. program—which stands for Conservation, Utilization, Reforestation, and Education, the four major components of good forest management. IHPA also acts as industry advisor to the U.S. delegation to the International Tropical Timber Organization and fully supports that organization's efforts to promote cooperation between producers and consumers of tropical timber.

7

Corporate Agreements Can Protect Rainforest Species

Elissa Blum

Elissa Blum was a student at Princeton University's Woodrow Wilson School of Public and International Affairs in Princeton, New Jersey, when this article was originally published. She is now a student at Harvard University Medical School in Boston.

Contractual agreements between biotechnology and pharmaceutical companies and countries that are rich in tropical rainforests can be helpful in the effort to identify, use, and preserve millions of rainforest species. Such agreements benefit the companies involved by streamlining the search for useful chemicals and by protecting the companies' property rights. They benefit the participating countries by generating revenues for cataloguing species and conserving forests.

> "This land is the place where we know where to find all that it provides for us—food from hunting and fishing, and farms, building and tool materials, medicines. This land keeps us together within its mountains; we come to understand that we are not just a few people or separate villages, but one people belonging to a homeland."
> —*The Akawaio Indians, Upper Mazaruni District, Guyana*[1]

Like the Akawaio Indians of Guyana, all of the world's human population depends on biological diversity for sustained development. Natural resources provide agricultural products for food, fiber for clothes, timber for fuel and construction, and chemicals for medicinal uses. Forests protect soils from decay and absorb carbon dioxide from the environment. Insects and microorganisms, many too small to be seen by the naked eye, process wastes, renew soils, and provide nutrients for plants.[2]

All of these resources are threatened, however, because biological diversity is decreasing at an ever-increasing rate—even faster than rates of evolutionary replacement.[3] Resources and species are being exploited and

From Elissa Blum, "Making Biodiversity Conservation Profitable," *Environment*, vol. 35, no. 4, pp. 16-20, 38-45, September 1993. Reprinted with permission of the Helen Dwight Reid Educational Foundation. Published by Heldref Publications, 1319 18th St. NW, Washington, DC 20036-1802. Copyright ©1993.

destroyed without regard to their long-term value. If people continue to exploit biological diversity as they have in the past, humans in the future will not be able to depend on natural resources. Clearly, methods to conserve biological diversity must be devised and implemented. All populations must find ways to ensure the sustainable use of biological resources by balancing present developmental progress with the needs of future generations.

One method by which this balance could be achieved is through the proliferation of agreements such as the one between Merck & Company and the Instituto Nacional de Biodiversidad in Costa Rica (INBio). According to the terms of a September 1991 agreement, INBio collects and processes plant, insect, and soil samples in Costa Rica and gives them to Merck for evaluation as prospective medicines. The contract provides Costa Ricans with an economically beneficial alternative to deforestation and concurrently advances the research efforts of Merck. Are agreements like the one between Merck and INBio a solution to the perceived incompatibility of economic growth and biodiversity preservation within developing nations? Before considering the collaborative agreement, it is first necessary to understand why biodiversity preservation is a problem.

Preserving biodiversity

Biological diversity, "the variety among living organisms and the ecological communities they inhabit," consists of three categories, or levels: genetic diversity, species diversity, and ecosystem diversity.[4] Species diversity, the level most often studied, is defined as the extant number and variety of species of plants, animals, fungi, microorganisms, and other living beings.

It has been estimated that between 5 million and 30 million species exist; most biologists regard 10 million as the best approximation. Only 1.4 million of these species have been named by taxonomists. Tropical forests, predominantly in Central and South America and Southeast Asia, contain from 50 to 90 percent of all species, including two-thirds of all vascular plant species and up to 96 percent of insect species. At current deforestation rates, it is estimated that between 4 and 8 percent of all rain forest species would be in danger of extinction by 2015, and from 17 to 35 percent would be in danger of extinction by 2040.[5]

Why is so much of the world's biodiversity in danger of destruction? One of the prime reasons is the incompatibility of short-term economic growth with the sustainable development of natural resources. When an economically struggling country has a choice between logging a forest to sell timber for high profits and leaving the forest intact without monetary compensation, the nation usually chooses the profitable alternative. Because immediate economic gains to the nation are more important than future environmental costs, deforestation occurs without regard to its long-term effects on biodiversity preservation.

This type of destructive activity occurs because the environment is a market externality; because no economic gain or loss is recorded in a basic accounting network when biological resources are used, the resources are considered to be free.[6] Externalities occur when there are no formal ownership rights to a good. Because it is difficult for a country to realize profitable returns from the environment, many nations are averse to expending large sums of money to preserve it.

Despite previous failures of the market to preserve biodiversity, market reform offers nations the best incentive to sustain their natural resources. According to Jessica T. Mathews, a vice president of the World Resources Institute (WRI) in Washington, D.C., the "marketplace is the most efficient way to achieve [positive] environmental ends . . . if you can make the marketplace work."[7] To make it work, countries must find ways to make resource conservation more profitable than resource exploitation. They can only do so by expressing sovereignty over their natural resources, accepting the responsibility to conserve them, and limiting access to those who abide by certain regulations.[8]

The [INBio] contract provides Costa Ricans with an economically beneficial alternative to deforestation.

The first step toward this type of natural resource control was taken at a summit in Managua, Nicaragua, on 6 June 1992. At this meeting, the presidents of Belize, Costa Rica, El Salvador, Guatemala, Honduras, Nicaragua, and Panama signed a nonbinding resolution that encouraged the passage of laws to regulate and restrict the extraction of natural resources from their countries. The goal of the resolution was to prevent foreigners from invading their nations' wildlands and extracting valuable resources without compensating the host nation.[9]

The presidents were motivated to sign the agreement by the realization that foreign companies, especially biotechnology and pharmaceutical firms, were using Central America's natural resources to develop drugs from which Central Americans realized no profits. The case of the Madagascar periwinkle is often cited as the prime example of this problem. The multimillion dollar cancer drug vincristine was developed from natural resources extracted from the Madagascar periwinkle, and yet Madagascar received no payment or share of the royalties.[10] Other countries have been exploited as well; WRI estimated that Costa Rica has lost more than $4 billion during the past 20 years from unrealized returns on natural resources.[11]

Prior to this resolution, no Central American country had ever passed laws regulating the extraction of biological resources. Now, many of these countries have made a commitment to do so. According to the Central American Commission on the Environment and Development, laws enacted by individual nations under this resolution should include guidelines for extraction of resources, payment of royalties from products developed from biological resources, future access to patents on the resources, rules ensuring the transfer of technology to the host country, access to advanced research materials, and rules for sharing the expertise necessary to market the developed products.[12]

Exploiting natural resources

The need for developing countries to assert sovereignty over their natural resources arose in part because of the extraction of resources by biotechnology and pharmaceutical companies for commercial development. Biotechnology, "the science of recombining the genes of plants and organisms to derive improved plants, drugs, and foods," has revolutionized ways in which natural resources are used in product development.[13] Prior to the 1950s, drugs were often developed from natural resources. However, they were discovered in a haphazard and time-intensive manner. From the 1950s to the 1980s, pharmaceutical companies found that synthetic chemicals and genetic engineering were more profitable than screening plants. Therefore, natural resource research slowed. Recently, however, the drug discovery process has reverted to more traditional methods. The usefulness of natural resources in drugs is derived in part from the fact that tropical plants often have strong chemical defenses to repel predators.[14] Although the more simple of these compounds have been synthesized in the laboratory, pharmaceutical companies are realizing that it would be impossible to replicate all of nature's more complex compounds. By using new bioassays and technology to test natural resources, the identification of certain natural resources as prospective drugs has become easier and more accurate. Thus, the drug discovery process has moved back into the rain forest and so increased the number of reasons to exploit the environment.[15]

Biotechnology and pharmaceutical companies also have an incentive not to exploit the environment, however, because doing so would eliminate one of their prime research bases. Traditional medicines, which are derived from natural resources, form the basis of health care for approximately 80 percent of the populations of developing nations.[16] Chances are good that, among the 10 million or so unidentified species in the rain forests, "there's something in there that can do everything we want done."[17] The destruction of biodiversity would mean the destruction of unique chemicals that may not be replicable in the laboratory.[18] Although the number of drugs developed directly from natural resources may be small, it has been estimated that one-quarter of all medicinal prescriptions in the United States are based in some way upon plants or microbes or are synthetic chemicals derived from them.[19] Examples of drugs derived from natural resources include penicillin, developed from a mold; taxol, a cancer drug from yew tree bark; and the antibiotic streptomycin, developed from a soil sample.[20]

The biodiversity convention

The seeming incompatibility of extracting natural resources for profits and protecting biological diversity within the tropics was one of the prime concerns of the representatives negotiating the Biodiversity Convention at the Earth Summit in Rio de Janeiro in June 1992. The treaty developed at the conference was designed to ensure the use of biological diversity in a sustainable way and to put guidelines into place that would make economic use of natural resources more compatible with their conservation. The United States was one of the few nations that participated in the summit but did not sign the treaty.[21]

One of the main reasons why the United States refused to sign the treaty was because it did not seem to protect intellectual property rights to the extent that biotechnology and pharmaceutical companies desired.

The United States—the world leader in the commercial development of biotechnology products, whose annual sales are expected to reach $50 billion by 2000—feared that the vague language of the treaty would be interpreted in such a way that the United States would lose its comparative advantage in the field.[22] The treaty sections most highly contested by biotechnology companies include paragraphs 15 and 16, which they felt would let developing countries make wide exclusions from intellectual property protection and would permit them to enact laws with overly broad compulsory licensing clauses.[23] The drug firms feared that these laws could force them to transfer patent rights to a new drug to a developing country.

The Merck/INBio agreement

The type of contractual agreement that many hope would be encouraged by the biodiversity treaty is exemplified by the agreement between Merck & Company, the world's largest pharmaceutical company, and the Instituto Nacional de Biodiversidad in Costa Rica. The agreement, announced on 19 September 1991, is a two-year "collaborative research agreement" under which Merck agreed to pay INBio a sum of $1 million for all of the plant, insect, and soil samples the institute could collect in addition to a percentage of the royalties from any drugs that Merck develops from samples provided by INBio.[24] The royalties, which were estimated to be in the range of 1 to 3 percent but were not made known to the public, will be split equally between INBio and the Costa Rican Ministry of Natural Resources.[25]

The drug discovery process has moved back into the rain forest and so increased the number of reasons to exploit the environment.

Under the agreement, Merck gets exclusive rights, called "right of first refusal," to evaluate the approximately 10,000 samples that INBio agreed to supply to Merck.[26] INBio may enter into similar agreements with other parties, but it must not supply the same species samples that it supplies to Merck unless given explicit permission to do so.[27]

According to Thomas Eisner, an entomologist at Cornell University, "The agreement is a win-win situation. It protects the proprietary rights of the industry, while at the same time recognizing that it is to the advantage of industrial nations to help with the custodianship of natural resources."[28] Merck benefits from the contract by receiving a limited number of plant, insect, and soil samples, already identified and classified. Because the samples are extracted and processed before they reach the Merck laboratories, Merck can immediately focus upon testing the samples for chemical activity.[29] The agreement specifies that, if Merck discovers any active ingredients from which it develops commercial products, the company will retain all patent rights to the developed product.[30] According to Georg Albers-Schonberg, executive director of Merck's Natural Products Division, Merck is skeptical about achieving immediate results from chemical prospecting. If not for the agreement, however, regions containing potential drugs would be destroyed, and the prospect of discovering an active ingredient for a drug would decrease even further.[31]

INBio and Costa Rica benefit from the agreement as well. One of the most important yet least tangible of the benefits incurred by Costa Rica is the ability to use its natural resources in a sustainable way while concurrently strengthening the Costa Rican economy. If INBio can create more jobs, profits, and a better-educated constituency by cataloging and selling rights to the country's natural resources than by destroying its resources, it makes economic sense to keep the resources intact.[32] On the more tangible side, in addition to the $1 million from Merck, INBio has benefited from technology transfer in the form of equipment donations worth $135,000 to carry out the chemical extraction process. Merck supplied INBio with two natural products chemists to set up the extraction laboratories and to train scientists in the purification techniques. Costa Rican scientists are also permitted to visit certain Merck laboratories if they wish to learn more. Eventually, INBio hopes that the training will aid Costa Rica in developing its own biotechnology industry so that drug discovery can take place entirely within national boundaries.[33]

The royalties that INBio receives from Merck will be used to support the conservation of Costa Rica's biodiversity. Ten percent of the initial $1 million plus 50 percent of the royalties go directly to Costa Rica's Ministry of Natural Resources; the rest of the profits are used to preserve the environment at the discretion of INBio and its board of directors.[34] The prospect of royalties from commercially developed products could have a drastic effect on Costa Rica's economy. According to the World Resources Institute, if INBio receives 2 percent of the royalties from the sale of 20 products based on its samples, INBio would receive more money than Costa Rica does from the sale of coffee and bananas, two prime exports.[35] This money could be used to build a Costa Rican biotechnology industry and to strengthen Costa Rica's economy.

Developing the agreement

The idea for the agreement developed from the technique of chemical prospecting, "the exploratory process by which new, useful natural products are discovered."[36] Chemical prospecting, a term coined by Thomas Eisner, involves three processes: first, natural resources are screened for their chemical or biochemical activity; second, the active components within the natural resources are isolated and characterized; and third, the active components are screened for certain activity.[37] Eisner believes that, by shifting chemical screening from industry to the nation in which the resource is located, an incentive could be created to preserve the natural environment.[38] Linking the biological inventorying that already occurs in tropical nations by institutes such as INBio to chemical prospecting would also decrease the randomness of the screening process. A person searching for a plant with a certain type of chemical repellent could look in the inventory catalog for plants that are free of certain kinds of insects and screen those plants rather than plants randomly selected from the rain forest. This link would hasten the identification of potentially useful medicines and other plant- and insect-based products and would not hinder efforts at conserving the environment; industries that find a useful chemical within a natural resource would try to replicate synthetically the chemical structure of the active component of the resource within the laboratory rather than continue to isolate it from the actual resource.[39]

Eisner's plan makes money for the countries in which the resources are located and motivates them to preserve rather than destroy their environment. The resource-rich nations could form alliances with universities and industries for certain up-front or royalty-based fees to insure that some of the profits from commercialization are captured by the country that initially located, cataloged, and screened the natural resource. Local residents could be trained to carry out the chemical screening to give them an alternative to environmentally destructive sources of employment and to strengthen the science base of their country.[40]

Resource-rich nations could form alliances with universities and industries for certain up-front or royalty-based fees.

Eisner has suggested that, to finance the prospecting, foundations, universities, government laboratories, and industry should all support the developing nations with money, materials, and scientific training in varying degrees. Because it would be laboratories within these institutions that would benefit from the more accurate and faster screening process, these institutions should support developing nations in their efforts.[41] In addition, debt-for-nature swaps, by which indebted countries can convert some of their debt into local investments to preserve the environment, could help finance the screening process.[42]

Because of his idea for institutional support of chemical prospecting, Eisner called Paul Anderson, vice president of medicinal chemistry at Merck Sharp & Dohme Research Laboratories, to suggest that Merck support INBio with a grant. Anderson met with Eisner and realized that there was potential for more direct cooperation. Lynn Caporale, of Merck's Academic & Industry Relations Department, was familiar with Costa Rica and felt that a more direct agreement would be in accord with Merck's high level of research and previous success with finding drugs from natural resources.[43] Merck had already developed many products based upon environmental samples. In the 1940s, Merck helped develop the antibiotic streptomycin from a soil sample. In the 1940s and 1950s, Merck made two major natural resource discoveries: Vitamin B-12, useful for treatment of pernicious anemia, was found in a fermentation broth, and mevalonic acid, a link in the body's synthesis of cholesterol, was discovered in a yeast extract. Based upon these successes, Merck developed natural resource screening techniques and discovered the drugs Mefoxin, Primaxin, and Mevacor.[44]

During a conference in October 1990 with Eisner, Anderson, and Rodrigo Gamez of the University of Costa Rica, the idea for the cooperative, profit-sharing agreement between Merck and INBio was solidified.[45] Others instrumental to the success of the agreement were Daniel Janzen, of the University of Pennsylvania, and Bob Bisset, senior director of corporate licensing at Merck and Merck's lead negotiator of the deal.[46] The specifics of the agreement are that the soil samples collected by INBio are sent directly to Merck's lab in Madrid, Spain, for analysis. The plant and insect samples are frozen and chemically extracted in a partnership with the University of Costa Rica. INBio supplies Merck with a list of the cataloged and classified plant and insect samples, from which Merck may choose a limited number to receive and test. These specific extracts are sent to Merck laboratories, where they are run through various bioassays to test for activity against certain receptors or enzymes known to be associated with specific diseases.[47] Paul Anderson, Georg Albers-Schonberg, and Keith Bostian, Merck's executive director of microbiology and molecular genetics, head the screening effort once the chemicals are sent to Merck. The laboratories of senior research microbiologist Gerald Bills, senior research fellow George Garrity, research fellow Robert B. Borris, and staff chemist Keith Witherup work on the identification of potential drugs from the natural resource samples.[48]

Although it may take a few years before Merck finds any commercially marketable chemicals within the natural resources supplied by INBio, the company does hope to make more discoveries through the collaborative agreement than through the more random screening processes, which currently are estimated to yield just one drug discovery from every 10,000 samples. Even if Merck does not find any active chemicals in usable form in INBio's natural resource samples, the company may find an extract that can be chemically modified to form a marketable product.[49]

A unique situation?

The agreement between Merck and INBio would not have been possible if INBio and Costa Rica had not had certain distinct characteristics, such as the technical expertise in Costa Rica to process samples, a transportation system to speed them to Merck Sharp & Dohme Research Laboratories in the United States and Spain, a scientific collection system already in place, and an established Merck network through the facilities of the Merck Manufacturing and Merck Human Health Divisions in Costa Rica.[50]

Costa Rica's high level of dedication to preserving its biodiversity and vast supply of natural resources put it in a unique position to negotiate agreements with foreign firms. More than one-quarter of Costa Rica's land is protected in some type of national park or preserve.[51] It is estimated that Costa Rica contains 12,000 plant species, 80 percent of which have been described, and 300,000 insect species, only 20 percent of which have been described.[52] Scientists estimate that Costa Rica is home to between 5 and 7 percent of the world's species and has more biological diversity per acre than any other nation. This vast species variability is due to the diverse climates within Costa Rica; the country is mountainous, touches both the Atlantic and Pacific oceans, and has ecosystems representative of South America, the West Indies, and tropical North America.[53] Costa Rica's government is stable and democratic, and its population is extremely well educated (the government estimates a 98-percent adult literacy), and yet it still faces many of the same economic pressures that often force developing nations to succumb to sacrificing environmental protection for more profitable endeavors.[54]

To prevent environmental deterioration, Hernan Bravo, Costa Rica's minister of natural resources, says, the National Assembly is working on developing a Wildlife Conservation Law to give the government the ability to negotiate with foreign firms that desire to use materials from Costa Rica's environment. This would be the first law of its kind in Central America and is expected to be passed and enacted by the end of the year. Other Central American countries plan to follow suit in accordance with the resolution that they signed in Nicaragua in June 1992. According to Bravo, the law will guarantee that companies that invest their technology and expertise in Costa Rica in exchange for natural resources will not be forced to turn over product patents and abundant profits far into the future but, rather, will be bound to abide by mutually agreed-upon contracts similar to the one signed by Merck and INBio.[55]

INBio has attempted to improve environmental education and expand the scientific work force among Costa Ricans.

Another unique characteristic of Costa Rica that makes it appealing as a partner in agreements with foreign firms is the stature of INBio. INBio is a nonprofit, private, scientific organization founded in 1989 according to recommendations by the Costa Rican government. Initially designed by Daniel Janzen and Rodrigo Gamez, INBio was instituted to study biodiversity and its socioeconomic value as a way to demonstrate the economic benefits of natural resource preservation.[56] The institute, now directed by Gamez, inventories and catalogs Costa Rica's biological diversity and prepares a computer database of species names, conservation status, distribution, abundance, way of life, and potential uses in medicine, agriculture, and industry. The cost of inventorying all of Costa Rica's species is estimated at $50 million, which will be spent over the 10 years that, INBio approximates, it will take to complete the inventory.[57] INBio hopes that some of this money will come from agreements, such as the one with Merck, and eventually from royalties. Additional funding for the inventory has been supplied by a debt-for-nature swap, local and international grants, development assistance, and private foundations.[58]

To raise funds with its biodiversity catalog, INBio has been developing various arrangements that, it hopes, will lead to cooperative agreements with foreign firms, organizations, or governments. One arrangement, called "the lottery" by Ana Sittenfeld, director of research and development for INBio, consists of INBio providing the foreign firm with a predetermined number of coded compounds. If the company finds a commercial use for the compound and desires more of it, the firm must agree to share a certain percentage of the royalties with INBio before the source of the compound is revealed. This scheme will work because of a bar-code system; because the company does not know the name of the species it is testing until INBio agrees to reveal this information, it cannot circumvent INBio and go directly to the environment to collect more of the beneficial sample. A second possible type of arrangement for cooperation would follow a request by a foreign firm for samples of compounds that exhibit certain characteristics, such as species that exhibit a resistance to certain types of insects or fungal infections. In each type of agreement, INBio contends that it will permit the company to keep the patent rights to any commercially developed products as long as INBio receives royalties that it can use to conserve Costa Rica's environment.[59] All funds received by INBio, above operating costs, are placed in a special fund managed in cooperation with the Costa Rican government to ensure that the money is directed to conservation activities.[60]

In addition to cataloging Costa Rica's biodiversity, INBio has attempted to improve environmental education and expand the scientific work force among Costa Ricans. According to Gamez, economic measures to improve the environment, such as the Merck/INBio agreement, are not enough to preserve biodiversity; cultural and intellectual measures must be adopted as well so that the people understand the importance of the environment.[61] To train workers to identify and collect samples for its database, INBio administers a six-month course in parataxonomy, including classes in botany, entomology, and ecology. More than 30 laypeople interested in environmental conservation have been trained so far to collect, dry, pin, and box Costa Rica's species.[62] During the first six months after the first class of parataxonomists was trained, more than four times as many insect samples were collected as had been placed in Costa Rica's insect collection during the previous 100 years.[63]

Response to the agreement

Acclaim for the Merck/INBio agreement has been widespread, with representatives of environmental groups, developing nations, biotechnology and pharmaceutical firms, and the U.S. government supporting the unique endeavor. Roberto Rojas, Costa Rica's minister of foreign trade, contends that the deal with Merck was very good. . . . We do think we need protection because we know we can serve as a vehicle for providing profits to companies, but that deal was satisfactory for us."[64] Lee Claro, from Upjohn Pharmaceutical's Washington, D.C., office, thinks that the deal was admirable, as well.[65]

There are some people, however, who do not think that the agreement was the best one that could have been made. Various people have said that they are skeptical about the deal because the actual agreement has not been released.[66] Rodrigo Gamez says that certain parts of the deal, such as the exact percentage of the royalties, were not made public to prevent other inventorying organizations from underpricing INBio in an effort to steal their business.[67] Costa Rican Congresswoman Brigitte Adler feels that INBio may have sold off Costa Rica's natural resources too cheaply.[68] But INBio is selling a product whose returns are uncertain; Merck may discover no prospective products from the agreement and may have paid $1 million for nothing, or it may discover 10 prospective drugs that could yield the company millions. INBio has responded to some people's expressed fear that it would gain in some way from the agreements rather than use all the profits to preserve biodiversity, by saying that most such fears have been caused by a misunderstanding of INBio's intent. Costa Rica's Ministry of Natural Resources has already received the first installment of Merck's fee to INBio, which will be used to support a marine park on Coco Island, off of Costa Rica.[69] In response to the fear that the agreement will fail to protect the environment because it depends on the work of INBio rather than on the work of the local population, Thomas Eisner contends that the deal does involve the local population; it trains parataxonomists, increases the environmental education efforts, and encourages the seven regional national park management bodies to increase local participation in decisionmaking.[70]

The impact of the treaty

Although most scientists, environmentalists, and government officials feel that the Merck/INBio agreement is the type of contract that they would like to see come out of the biodiversity treaty, differing opinions exist regarding the feasibility of such agreements under the treaty in its current form. Eisner thinks that deals like the Merck/INBio agreement would occur anyway but would be facilitated by both countries being party to the treaty. The United States' refusal to sign the treaty is detrimental, Eisner believes: "We lose by not signing that treaty, although as in the first throes of any agreement, some wording needs to be refined. [International collaborations] are going to happen whether we sign or not, but the goodwill attendant to having signed would have put the United States in a much better position to approach these developing countries."[71] Kenton Miller of WRI feels that certain countries, such as Venezuela, might refuse to work with the United States because, by not signing, it did not state its intentions to preserve its own biodiversity. These nations will not cooperate with countries they think might take advantage of them.[72]

Others feel that the biodiversity treaty as it exists would preclude agreements like that which was signed by Merck and INBio. According to Richard Godown, president of the International Biotechnology Association, "The convention would tie the hands of negotiators: When they sat down to make a deal there would be an enormous slug of mandatory contract language. . . . It would result in a bum deal."[73] Godown fears that the treaty is too specific regarding the terms of cooperation and technology transfer and that it would prevent contracting parties from negotiating the best possible terms based upon the specific nature of each situation.

However, Richard Wilder, an intellectual property rights lawyer in Washington, D.C., and a member of the Association of Biotechnology Companies' patent committee, says that, from a legal standpoint, there is nothing in the treaty that would prevent the Merck/INBio agreement.[74] The treaty does not require any certain type of contract. Rather, its vague language can be interpreted by different parties to support different agreements with varying levels of intellectual property rights. What the biotechnology and pharmaceutical companies fear is that developing nations will interpret the vague language as supporting weak intellectual property protection, while industry will interpret the vague language as supporting the opposite position.

According to Eisner, "The INBio deal should be a blueprint for other countries to follow. It is a way to provide economic growth along with protecting our precious biological diversity."[75] And, indeed, while the U.S. government is waiting to solve the dilemma over the signing of the treaty, other cooperative research agreements similar to the one between

Merck and INBio are being set up.[76] Other pharmaceutical companies are studying the agreement, and other developing countries, including China, Chile, Mexico, India, Indonesia, Nepal, and Nicaragua, are investigating INBio in an effort to set up similar institutions in their own nations.[77] However, Walter Reid at WRI cautions that INBio as it exists in Costa Rica may not be an appropriate model for other countries. Costa Rica is unique in that it has a stable democratic government and a well-known commitment to preserving biodiversity. Other nations may abandon other efforts at conservation in hope of large economic profits from prospecting agreements or may not really use the profits derived from their inventories for resource conservation. In an effort to prevent this type of exploitation of an otherwise positive conservation mechanism, Reid is working with INBio, the Rainforest Alliance, and the African Center for Technology Studies to create guidelines for future prospecting agreements and institutions.[78]

Each new INBio-like institution would have to be adapted to the unique culture, environment, and political climate of its nation. For example, because India is composed largely of community-owned land and vast state-owned forests, such an institution within India would probably have to be decentralized. Indonesia, which already has a national genetic resources institute, may only need an information management system and a group of parataxonomists to establish a prospecting institute. Because Indonesia, India, Brazil, and Mexico each have their own pharmaceutical industries, cooperative agreements could take place nationally as well as internationally.[79] In nations without a government stable enough to support a prospecting and screening institute, previously established institutions in politically stable countries, such as INBio in Costa Rica, could expand their scope and catalog other nations' resources.[80]

Other developing countries . . . are investigating INBio in an effort to set up similar institutions in their own nations.

Other types of market-based natural resource exchange programs have been taking place alongside the Merck/INBio agreement, and it is likely that characteristics of some of these agreements would be useful in designing a unique prospecting establishment for each resource-rich nation. Shaman Pharmaceuticals Inc., a small California pharmaceutical firm founded in 1989 by Lisa Conte, is bypassing institutional mechanisms and going directly to native shamans (medicine men) in Brazil and Argentina to isolate traditional plant-derived medicines. According to Conte, "We are using the traditional use of plants as a prioritisation tool to have a more efficient process of drug discovery. By using traditional knowledge there is a greater likelihood of yielding an active compound or a pharmaceutical."[81] Shaman compensates the "ethnobotanists" who help Conte discover drugs by helping them to preserve the rain forests; in addition, if the company needs very large quantities of a plant, it pays people from the local communities to harvest it. A percentage of the company's profits are devoted to the Healing Forest Conservancy, a nonprofit organization founded by Conte to preserve the rain forest and assist indigenous peoples.[82] Conte contends that, by using the native shamans in the search for drugs, "We are creating an economical alternative to the destruction of the rain forest. If they can make a living by collecting our products, it gives them an incentive for leaving the forests intact."[83] Her company has already had a high level of success with its drug discovery process; two of its drugs are now undergoing clinical tests. One is the antiviral agent Provir, useful for treating respiratory infections and herpes 1 and 2, and the other is an antifungal agent useful for treating certain fungal infections.[84]

In another cataloging effort, the U.S. National Cancer Institute in Bethesda, Maryland, is at work creating a repository of natural resource specimens. It has renewed two five-year contracts with the Missouri and New York botanical gardens, whose botanists collect samples that may be viable treatments for cancer or AIDS. The institute is currently working on a "material transfer agreement" under which it will share some of its profits with governments or departments in the countries in which it prospects.[85]

Policy recommendations

Over the past 20 years, the United States has enacted much state and federal legislation addressing specific aspects of biodiversity. It never, until the Earth Summit, addressed the issue of comprehensive biodiversity legislation.[86] To rectify this situation, the government should undertake a number of initiatives. First, the United States should sign the biodiversity treaty to demonstrate its positive intent to preserve the environment.

Not all interested parties feel that signing the treaty in its current form is in the best interest of the United States. Both the Industrial Biotechnology Association and the Association of Biotechnology Companies pressured President George Bush to withhold his signature from the treaty. The trade associations reaffirmed their support of biodiversity conservation but expressed dismay at the process and outcome of the convention. According to Walter Reid, "When you talk to people who were on the U.S. delegation [in Rio], by and large what they say is [that] nobody was talking to them at all about the [biodiversity] treaty, from the environmental community to the biotech industry. There was virtually no attention being given to [the treaty], much to our frustration."[87]

Richard Wilder says that biotechnology companies have rational reasons for opposing the treaty: "I think that the language the way it is now provides the possibility . . . for countries either to decide not to provide intellectual property protection for biotechnology or to dilute it through very broad compulsory licensing provisions, either possibility of which would be damaging to the biotech industry, which depends upon having strong intellectual property protection to develop new technologies . . . and, once it's developed, to transfer it or to otherwise make use of it."[88]

Others, however, feel that the United States should have signed the treaty to show its good intentions and then worked with the flawed language to make it more appealing to U.S. industry. Although article 37 of the treaty states that no country can sign it with reservations to certain clauses, many of the signatories, including Italy, France, and England, signed the treaty and stated the way in which they will interpret its vague clauses.[89] Kenton Miller thinks that the United States should "join with other countries after we sign [the treaty] in sponsoring continuing negotiating meetings to look at those aspects that are indeed far from clear. . . . From a Supreme Court point of view, we ought to have it all clear before we sign it, but in most countries they don't hold to that rigor. . . . So [not signing because of the vague language] made us sort of stand out."[90]

Although certain aspects of the treaty do merit clarification, this is not reason enough for the United States to withhold its signature from the treaty. The U.S. government must prove its determination to work with other nations to preserve biodiversity. Therefore, it should sign the treaty and issue a statement delineating how it interprets the vague articles, especially articles 15 and 16. The government should then meet with representatives from environmental groups, biotechnology and pharmaceutical firms, and nongovernmental organizations to determine the best possible ways to modify the treaty. Alterations to the treaty should focus upon using the market, rather than legislation, to promote biodiversity preservation. Changes should be made to permit and encourage market agreements like the Merck/INBio agreement, without infringing upon the right of individual parties to negotiate contracts and intellectual property rights on a case-by-case basis. These improvements should be proposed to all signatories at the general meeting to be held in Nairobi in August 1993. Because this meeting will be held prior to the treaty ratification deadline, the United States may be able to renegotiate the treaty to suit its interests before the issue is brought up before Congress.

Changes should be made to permit and encourage market agreements like the Merck/INBio agreement.

In addition to signing the biodiversity treaty, the United States should encourage the legal adoption of the guidelines currently in development for designing INBio-like institutions internationally. Such guidelines could be attached as an appendix to the biodiversity treaty or could constitute a separate agreement. The United States should take a leading role in promoting such institutions by becoming one of the first countries to institute a national biodiversity prospecting center to collect and catalog its own biodiversity. Such a center has already been proposed as part of the National Biodiversity Conservation Act drafted by David Blockstein during his fellowship in Representative James H. Scheuer's (D-N.Y.) office in 1987 and 1988.[91]

Each national biodiversity prospecting center should catalog its inventory on a database. A brief summary of the content of each of these databases should be compiled by the U.N. Environment Programme and made available to industrial groups internationally. Each party should be able to negotiate its own agreements based upon certain requirements, including the fair transfer of natural resources, the commitment to use the resources in a nondestructive way, and the equitable payment of a certain level of start-up expenses and royalties. The existence of a number of these prospecting centers would provide enough incentive to abide by the guidelines; any establishment that tried to subvert the regulations would lose its customers to another nation's biodiversity center.

If these policy recommendations were instituted, developing nations would be able to resolve the seeming incompatibility of sustained economic growth and environmental preservation. Merck/INBio-like agreements represent a profitable alternative to deforestation and provide nations with a greater incentive to preserve their biodiversity than is provided by any type of legislative action or regulation. Thus, the enactment and enforcement of these policy recommendations would help preserve the world's biodiversity. They cannot stand alone, however; environmental education must be improved both in the classroom and in society at large so that populations learn to value biodiversity as they value other national assets. The United States should foster scientific training and exchange programs with other nations to promote the flow of information and to heighten awareness of environmental issues.

Notes

1. World Resources Institute, World Conservation Union, and United Nations Environment Programme, *Global Biodiversity Strategy* (Washington, D.C.: WRI, 1992).

2. Council on Environmental Quality, *United States of America National Report* (Washington, D.C.: U.S. Government Printing Office, 1992), 292.

3. T. Eisner, "Chemical Prospecting: A Proposal for Action," in F.H. Bormann and S.R. Kellert, eds., *Ecology, Economics, Ethics: The Broken Circle* (New Haven, Conn.: Yale University Press, 1991), 196.

4. World Resources Institute, *World Resources 1992–93: A Guide to the Global Environment* (New York: Oxford University Press, 1992), 127–28.

5. Ibid., 127–31.

6. R. Repetto, Presentation at Princeton University, New Jersey, 26 October 1992.

7. J.T. Mathews, Presentation at Princeton University, New Jersey, 26 October 1992.

8. World Bank, *World Development Report 1992: Development and the Environment* (New York: Oxford University Press, 1992), 64.

9. *BNA International Environment Daily*, "Central American Presidents Resolve to Pass Laws Restricting Use of Resources," 11 June 1992.

10. C. Joyce, "Prospectors for Tropical Medicines," *New Scientist*, 19 October 1991, 36–40.

11. *Inter Press Service*, "Costa Rica: Plant Life Exploitation Rights Scheme 'A Bad Deal,'" 15 January 1992.

12. *BNA International Environment Daily*, "Central American Presidents to Sign Separate Accord on Biological Resources," 4 June 1992.

13. G. Browning, "Biodiversity Battle," *National Journal*, 8 August 1992, 1827.

14. Joyce, note 10 above, pages 37–38.

15. Ibid.; and L. Roberts, "Chemical Prospecting: Hope for Vanishing Ecosystems?" *Science* 256 (22 May 1992):1142–43.

16. World Resources Institute et al., note 1 above, page 4.

17. M. Mellon, Personal communication with the author, 20 October 1992.

18. Eisner, note 3 above, pages 196 and 199.

19. Joyce, note 10 above, pages 37–38.

20. G. Bylinsky, "The Race for a Rare Cancer Drug," *Fortune,* 13 July 1992, 100–02; Eisner, note 3 above, pages 197–98; and *Merck World,* "A Modern-Day Noah's Ark," no. 3 (1992).

21. K. Miller, Personal communication with the author and Peter Bartolino, 26 October 1992.

22. Browning, note 13 above.

23. *International Trade Reporter,* "Biodiversity Treaty Risks Interfering with Patent Protections, Official Says," 17 June 1992.

24. Merck & Co., "Summary of the INBio-Merck Agreement" (Unpublished memorandum, Rahway, N.J., September 1992); and idem, "INBio of Costa Rica and Merck Enter into Innovative Agreement to Collect Biological Samples While Protecting Rain Forest" (Press release, Rahway, N.J., 19 September 1991).

25. Roberts, note 15 above.

26. Ibid.; and J. Preston, "A Biodiversity Pact with a Premium," *Washington Post,* 9 June 1992, A16.

27. Merck & Co., "Summary," note 24 above.

28. T. Reynolds, "Drug Firms, Countries Hope to Cash in on Natural Products," *Journal of the National Cancer Institute* 84, no. 15 (5 August 1992):1147–48.

29. Merck & Co., "Summary," note 24 above.

30. *Pharmaceutical Business News,* "Pharmaceutical Companies Go 'Chemical Prospecting' for Medicines," 21 August 1992.

31. Joyce, note 10 above, page 39.

32. Merck & Co., "Searching for Medicines While Preserving the Rain Forest: The INBio/Merck Agreement" (Unpublished memorandum, Rahway, N.J., 12 May 1992).

33. Roberts, note 15 above.

34. Merck & Co., note 32 above.

35. World Resources Institute et al., note 1 above, page 152.

36. Eisner, note 3 above, page 196.

37. Ibid., page 199. The term *chemical prospecting* was first introduced in Reynolds, note 28 above.

38. T. Eisner, "Prospecting for Nature's Chemical Riches," *Issues in Science and Technology,* Winter 1989–90, 31–34.

39. Ibid.; and Eisner, note 3 above.

40. Eisner, note 3 above.

41. Eisner, note 38 above.

42. Eisner, note 3 above.

43. *Merck World,* note 20 above.

44. Ibid.

45. Roberts, note 15 above.

46. Joyce, note 10 above; and *Merck World,* note 20 above.

47. Roberts, note 15 above.

48. *Merck World,* note 20 above.

49. Roberts, note 15 above.

50. *Merck World,* note 20 above.

51. Joyce, note 10 above.

52. L. Tangley, "Cataloging Costa Rica's Diversity," *BioScience* 40, no. 9 (October 1990):633–36.

53. *Merck World,* note 20 above.

54. Ibid.; and Joyce, note 10 above.

55. *BNA International Environment Daily,* "New Measure Would Cover Extraction of Genetic Resources from Rain Forest," 21 July 1992.

56. Merck & Co., note 32 above; and Roberts, note 15 above.

57. Tangley, note 52 above.

58. World Resources Institute et al., note 1 above.

59. Joyce, note 10 above.

60. World Resources Institute et al., note 1 above.

61. Tangley, note 52 above.

62. Roberts, note 15 above; and Joyce, note 10 above.

63. World Resources Institute, note 4 above.

64. *BNA International Environment Daily,* note 55 above.

65. L. Claro, Personal communication with the author, 6 November 1992.

66. P. Juto, Presentation at Princeton University, New Jersey, 26 October 1992.

67. N. Adams, "Merck Drug to Pay Royalties on Costa Rican Forest," *National Public Radio Show: All Things Considered,* interview of Rodrigo Gamez, 10 June 1992.

68. *BNA International Environment Daily,* note 12 above.

69. Roberts, note 15 above.

70. P. Aldhous, "'Hunting Licence' for Drugs," *Nature* 353 (26 September 1991):290.

71. T. Eisner as quoted in T. Reynolds, "Biodiversity Treaty Still Unsigned by U.S.," *Journal of the National Cancer Institute* 84, no. 15 (5 August 1992): 1148.

72. Miller, note 21 above.

73. S. Usdin, "Biotech Industry Played Key Role in U.S. Refusal to Sign Bio-Convention," *Diversity* 8, no. 2 (1992):8–9.

74. R. Wilder, Personal communication with the author, 30 October 1992.

75. *BNA International Environment Daily,* "Deal Between Drug Firm, Costa Rica Called Example of What Treaty Would Do," 17 June 1992.

76. Joyce, note 10 above; and Miller, note 21 above.

77. Miller, note 21 above; Roberts, note 15 above; and Tangley, note 52 above.

78. Roberts, note 15 above.

79. Miller, note 21 above.

80. Ibid.

81. *Pharmaceutical Business News,* note 30 above.

82. *Industrial Bioprocessing,* "Back to Nature for Chemicals and Drugs," October 1991, 3.

83. *Pharmaceutical Business News,* note 30 above.

84. *Industrial Bioprocessing,* note 82 above; and *Pharmaceutical Business News,* note 30 above.

85. Joyce, note 10 above.

86. Council on Environmental Quality, note 2 above.

87. Browning, note 13 above.

88. Wilder, note 74 above.

89. Ibid.

90. Miller, note 21 above.

91. Tangley, note 52 above.

8

Sustainable Forestry Can Regenerate Mahogany Forests

Laura K. Snook

Laura K. Snook is a tropical forester and ecologist at Duke University in Durham, North Carolina. She has conducted research on mahogany ecology and silviculture on Mexico's Yucatan peninsula since 1987.

Mahogany is one of the largest and most valuable trees growing in the tropics. There are no longer any technological limits on the amount of mahogany that can be harvested. The best way to sustain the supply of mahogany is to re-create the natural conditions under which it regenerates and thrives.

Mahogany may be the most widely recognized and most popular of tropical woods, but until recently, the conditions required for its regeneration and growth were little understood. Native to the New World, mahogany is one of the largest trees in the tropical forest, attaining heights of about 70 meters and diameters in excess of 3 meters. In pre-Conquest America, the Maya made dugout canoes from mahogany trees, using them to transport goods up and down the coasts of Central America. The stability, durability and workability of mahogany timber drew the attention of European explorers like Sir Walter Raleigh, who used and praised it for ship repairs.

In the sixteenth century, the Spaniards took full advantage of the qualities of mahogany, using it in carved altars, furniture and ships. For the first 150 years, they focused on the so-called small-leaf, Caribbean or Cuban mahogany (*Swietenia mahagoni*) native to the Antilles, which was distinguished by narrow growth rings, tight grain and a deep red coloring. It didn't take long before the demand for this excellent timber exceeded the accessible supply on the islands, and in 1629 the Spanish navy established their principal shipyard on the mainland in what is now the state of Veracruz, Mexico. This location provided access to the more extensive resource of bigleaf or Honduras mahogany (*Swietenia macrophylla*), whose range extends from Mexico south through Central America, Venezuela and Colombia and across the southern Amazon basin.

From Laura K. Snook, "Mahogany: Mining vs. Management: No Limits to Extraction Remain." Reprinted, with permission, from *Understory* (vol. 7, no. 1, Fall/Winter 1997)—the quarterly journal of the Good Wood Alliance. For subscriptions or further information, contact: Good Wood Alliance, 289 College St., Burlington, VT 05401 (tel.: 802-899-1249; fax: 802-862-4448; e-mail: warp@together.net).

In the 1680s, the British, by agreement with the Spaniards, were permitted to log mahogany south of the Yucatan peninsula. There they established the logging settlements that became the colony of British Honduras (now Belize), importing black slaves from Africa to fell the huge trees with axes and drag them to rivers and lagoons whence they could be floated out to sea for export to England.

Technological constraints

From the 1500s to 1800, only mahogany trees near water could be harvested because manpower was not sufficient to haul logs more than a few hundred meters. Oxen were introduced to British Honduras in 1805 and could haul logs five miles to water. Later in the nineteenth century, narrow-gauge railroads were constructed to extract logs, and tracks were laid 30 kilometers or more into the forest. Crawler tractors, introduced in the 1920s, could penetrate even farther. By the 1950s, chainsaws, skidders with rubber tires and extensive logging roads overcame the last constraints to full access, making it possible to extract mahoganies from almost every part of the forest.

Technological limits protected the mahogany resource from depletion for 450 years. Not only was most of the forest inaccessible, but high standards for the export market meant that imperfect trees, or those less than enormous, were left behind. These trees provided the seed for new mahoganies. Today, there are no more technological limits to the rate or intensity of harvesting. Mahogany logging began in Pará, Brazil, in the 1960s and 70s, when heavy machinery was available for road construction. Since then, loggers have constructed more than 3,000 kilometers of roads, on which mahoganies are hauled as far as 500 km from the forest to the mills. Processing machinery can produce boards or veneer from small or imperfect trees.

Ecology and logging

In today's world, the only way to sustain mahogany is to implement silvicultural management. Silviculture is the art and science of regenerating desired species and favoring the development of forest stands that correspond to the management objectives of forest owners. (These may range from timber production to recreation, hunting or watershed protection.) The first step in developing silvicultural systems is understanding the ecology of the forest and of the species of interest.

Mahogany occurs in forests that are affected periodically by catastrophic disturbances. In Central America, hurricanes sweep through the region, occasionally knocking down trees over hundreds, or even thousands of hectares of forest. During the dry season, which lasts four to seven months, forest fires may start, either triggered by lightning or spreading from agricultural plots established by rural farmers who, over millennia, have used slash-and-burn techniques to grow corn in small forest openings. Fires are particularly common—and most intense—in years following hurricanes, when fallen leaves, twigs, branches and trees provide abundant fuel. In the Amazon River basin, crisscrossed with tributaries, logjams occasionally block the waterways, causing floods that may inundate thousands of hectares. These are the catastrophic events that allow mahogany to regenerate naturally in its native range.

Adult mahogany trees are well adapted to such disturbances. Their large buttressed roots and aerodynamic crowns enable the trees to survive hurricanes better than the dozens of other tree species in the forest, and their thick bark resists fire very well. Nor does mahogany seem to mind being flooded or buried to several meters in sediment. As a result, catastrophic disturbances tend to leave mahoganies standing in clearings produced by the destruction of hundreds of other trees that normally share each hectare. The surviving mahoganies shed their winged seeds on the bare land, and their seedlings emerge into the sunny conditions they require to survive and flourish. Other species seed in around them, and a new patch of forest, with as many as 50 mahoganies per hectare, begins to grow.

Today, there are no more technological limits to the rate or intensity of harvesting.

Between this time and the next disturbance, new mahogany trees will not become established because they cannot survive under the shade of the forest canopy. This means that all mahoganies over thousands of hectares are established at the same time—they're the same age. And since these catastrophic events only affect a given spot every few centuries, mahogany trees must endure for hundreds of years to have a chance to reproduce.

The conditions created by logging are the opposite of those produced by the natural disturbances described above. Loggers remove all the mahoganies of merchantable size—typically, all the mahoganies in a stand—and leave standing the hundreds of other trees, which have little, if any, market value. There are no young mahogany trees or seedlings in the understory, and after logging there are no seed sources. Even if seedlings were planted, as they sometimes are, they could not survive the lack of sunlight under the remaining canopy. As a result, mahogany logging is a mining operation; the resource is not renewed.

Silviculture and sustainability

What can we do to make mahogany a renewable resource? At the turn of the century, before the Amazonian mahogany reserves were discovered, concern about the depletion of this valuable species led foresters to establish mahogany plantations throughout Central America and as far afield as Java, Indonesia, and Fiji. Unfortunately, within the native range of mahogany, plantations were attacked by a shootboring insect (*Hypsipyla grandella*) that killed or deformed the trees, and the plantations were considered a failure. Outside the range of the pest, the Javanese and Fijian plantations are developing well, but they are just beginning to reach harvest size and they account for an insignificant portion of the international trade.

Within its native range, it seems that the best way to sustain mahogany is to try to imitate the natural conditions under which the species regenerates and grows so well: Start with a clearing and seeds, and let mahogany grow up among the other species that naturally seed in alongside it, where it is hidden from the shootborer. In Mexico and Belize, I am working with Maya communities, a Belizean organization and other scientists to test various methods of simulating the conditions produced by hurricane and fire. (Our research is funded by the European Union, World Wildlife Fund/Mexico and the USDA Forest Service, the Biodiversity Support Program and Duke University.) We are experimenting with four sizes of cleared plots, from 500 square meters to a half hectare, created by different clearing methods: slash-and-burn agriculture, bulldozers and logging. Within each clearing, we are seeding mahogany and planting seedlings. As we watch the new trees develop, we hope to discover which approach will be most successful for regenerating mahogany and most cost-effective to implement.

Unfortunately, we won't be able to use these practices on a commercial scale unless the timber economy can be made more favorable for sustainable management. In a global free market, a producer who invests in regeneration treatments must compete with mahogany timber mined without regard for the future from a retreating frontier of virgin forests. That is why voluntary and regulatory mechanisms like forest certification and listing on Appendix II of the Convention on International Trade in Endangered Species (CITES) are so important. Such instruments may not be able to transform mahogany logging from a mining process to sustainable management, but they are necessary to create a framework within which silviculture can be implemented.

Sustaining mahogany in natural forests will . . . provide a habitat for monkeys, tapirs and countless other animal and plant species.

Sustaining mahogany in natural forests will help ensure much more than a supply of high-quality timber for future generations. If mahogany forests can compete successfully with alternative land uses like cattle ranching and large-scale agriculture, they will also continue to provide a habitat for monkeys, tapirs and countless other animal and plant species, whose worth cannot be measured in board feet or dollars.

9

Logging Is Not a Threat to British Columbia's Rainforests

Forest Alliance of British Columbia

The Forest Alliance of British Columbia is a Canadian nonprofit organization in Victoria that seeks to protect British Columbia's forest environment and forest-based economy.

Clearcut logging is not a threat to British Columbia's temperate rainforests or its animal species. British Columbia's forest regulations—the strictest in the world—restrict the size and location of clearcuts and ensure that logging is conducted in an ecologically sound manner. Proper forestry practices, including replanting of clearcut areas, are preventing soil erosion, species extinction, and the loss of wildlife habitat and genetic diversity in British Columbia's rainforests.

A response to Greenpeace's European campaign of misinformation about British Columbia's [B.C.] forests.

In March 1994, the stump of a 400-year-old red cedar tree from Vancouver Island landed in Liverpool, England. Accompanied by Friends of Clayoquot Sound directors Valerie Langer and Garth Lenz and sponsored by Greenpeace U.K., "Stumpy" was the star attraction of a three week, 16-city tour of England and Scotland. The four-tonne stump was mounted on the back of a flatbed truck, driven from city to city, and displayed in town centres and public parks to promote Greenpeace's campaign to boycott B.C. forest product exports to Britain.

The Forest Alliance of B.C. was in Great Britain too, shadowing Stumpy and monitoring Greenpeace's public presentations. While Greenpeace has undertaken many well-founded environmental protests in the past, the campaign against B.C. forest practices was found to be wholly unsupported by scientific fact.

In its literature and its presentations, Greenpeace U.K. and the Friends of Clayoquot Sound presented a great many exaggerations, half-

From Forest Alliance of British Columbia, "What Greenpeace Isn't Telling Europeans," white paper, May 1994. Reprinted with permission.

truths and blatant falsehoods about British Columbia to the U.K. public.

The following represents the Forest Alliance team's effort to catalogue and respond to this campaign of misinformation. While the list is extensive, it is by no means exhaustive.

Clayoquot Sound on Canada's Vancouver Island in the province of British Columbia is one of the world's last remaining areas of ancient temperate rainforest.

Actually, about 8,400,000 hectares of ancient temperate rainforest remain intact along the coast of B.C. This represents about 80% of our province's original stands. But temperate rainforest also exists in other parts of the world, including Washington State, Oregon, northern California and South America.

Clayoquot Sound is by no means one of the world's last remaining areas of ancient temperate rainforest. It comprises about 2.5% of the total in B.C.

The majority of (B.C.) forest products are exported to Europe, the USA and Japan for use in newspapers, magazines, phone books, tissue paper and as timber.

In fact, about 92% of the trees harvested in B.C. are manufactured into solid wood products like lumber, plywood and roofing. The other 8% go directly into pulp and paper, but such trees generally have extensive rot or other conditions that make them inappropriate for solid wood manufacturing.

British Columbia's forest industry is structured primarily for the production of high-value solid wood building products. Pulp and paper manufacturing exists largely on the by-products of the sawmilling process.

An effective code

The 1994 Forest Practices Code is meant to ensure responsible logging, but is weak and unenforceable. It does not include any mechanisms for effective monitoring and explicitly allows clearcut logging.

Calling the Forest Practices Code weak and unenforceable while it was being developed highlights Greenpeace's opposition to logging in British Columbia under any terms.

The Code will provide greatly enhanced powers of enforcement, including on-the-spot stop-work and clean-up orders, fines of up to $1 million, and provisions for license suspensions and cut reductions. For the first time, government staff from two ministries (forests and environment) will take enforcement roles. Independent audits will be greatly enhanced and performance-based logging will be introduced, whereby approval of future logging activities is contingent upon past performance.

The Code will permit clearcut logging, but significantly restricts the size and location of clearcuts. This allowance explains Greenpeace's outright dismissal of the toughest forest practices legislation in the world, as the organization is opposed to clearcut logging in any form.

But in many of British Columbia's forests, properly managed clearcuts are recognized as the most ecologically appropriate harvesting system.

The Canadian rainforest . . . is made up of giant trees which can be up to 2,000 years old, stand up to 300 feet high and can be 60 feet around.

Some West Coast species trees do reach 800 years of age, and in the case of red cedar upwards of 1,000 years, but they are the exception rather than the rule. There's a wide distribution of tree ages within B.C.'s coastal old-growth forests, but the average age of canopy trees is 300 to 400 years.

Temperate rainforests have a higher bio-mass (the total weight of living organisms) than any other forest, including tropical rainforests.

Not true. Tropical rainforests have a higher bio-mass.

The mid-1950s saw the introduction of Tree Farm Licenses. In British Columbia, the province's forests (95% of the total) were parcelled up, and logging rights were given to a handful of large companies.

The [Forest Practices] Code will permit clearcut logging, but significantly restricts the size and location of clearcuts.

This is a misleading simplification of the forest tenure system in B.C. Tree Farm Licenses have never represented a large portion of the province. In 1994, they accounted for about 8% of B.C.'s land base; not 95% as Greenpeace claims.

The insistence that a "handful of large companies" control logging rights in B.C. is also misleading. The five largest logging companies currently possess 32% of the allowable annual cut. The top 10 possess 51%, and the top 20 possess 70%.

The percentage of allowable annual cut possessed by large forest companies has been steadily declining for 20 years.

The Forests Minister responsible for the introduction of these licenses was later imprisoned for four years for taking bribes.

Edward Kenney was B.C.'s Forests Minister when the tenure system was introduced in 1948. He was never accused, charged or imprisoned for accepting a bribe or for any other offense. A subsequent Forests Minister, Robert Sommers, was convicted in 1958 and sent to prison two years after leaving office.

In all, 95.6% of Vancouver Island's original ancient forest area has been logged or is scheduled to be logged. Only 4.4% is actually protected. . . . At current rates of logging, all will be gone by the year 2022.

It's incorrect to say all forest land not protected in parks is "scheduled to be logged." Hundreds of thousands of hectares of old-growth forest on Vancouver Island will never be logged for geographic reasons. Thousands more will never be logged because scenic, wildlife habitat and recreational values take priority.

There is absolutely no chance that Vancouver Island's old-growth forests will be gone by the year 2022.

The 4.4% figure for protected areas is also incorrect. About 10% of the temperate rainforest that originally blanketed Vancouver Island—and 20% of the remaining old-growth—is currently preserved as park.

Clayoquot Sound

Twenty-four per cent of the ancient forest in Clayoquot Sound has already been logged.

Just 13% of Clayoquot Sound has been logged over the past 100 years.

In total, 74% of Clayoquot Sound has already been clearcut or is earmarked for clearcutting.

Under the Clayoquot Sound land use plan, 62% of the region is theoretically open to logging. But because scenic, wildlife habitat and recreational values take priority in many areas, and other areas are inaccessible, B.C.'s chief provincial forester estimates only about 40% of the Clayoquot's forests will ever be logged.

The annual harvest in Clayoquot Sound is restricted to 1,000 hectares—less than one-half of 1% of the total forested area. All of it is replanted or managed for natural regeneration.

(The Scientific Panel for Sustainable Forest Practices in Clayoquot Sound) has already recommended that no further logging occur in intact areas in Clayoquot Sound. This recommendation has been ignored.

The independent panel referred to has made no such recommendation.

Fire is not an ecological function in temperate rainforests.

Forest fires do occur in coastal temperate rainforests, though with less frequency than in interior forests.

Greenpeace is implying that temperate rainforests do not suffer site disturbances as part of their natural life cycle. This is not the case. Fire, disease, insect infestation and more often wind storms provide natural site disturbances that stimulate forest regeneration. It is these events that forest managers attempt to mimic through clearcut logging.

In 1908, 30,000 hectares of temperate rainforest on Vancouver Island blew down in a single evening.

The Forest Practices Code places no legal limit on the size of clearcuts.

The Forest Practices Code has established explicit limits for clearcut size in each region and biogeoclimatic zone in the province. To impose one rigid standard on every forest would be ecologically inappropriate and detrimental to forest health.

Under the Code, clearcuts may not exceed 40 hectares on the coast and 60 hectares in the interior. Other provisions regulate clearcuts in relation to forest topography, nearby cutblocks and fish-bearing streams, lakes and other bodies of water.

Greenpeace ignores the fact that our forests would generate little or no economic activity without logging roads.

Clearcuts of up to 7,000 hectares are not uncommon in B.C., and legal under existing legislation.

Clearcuts of 7,000 hectares are extremely rare in B.C., and are usually employed to counter insect infestation or disease. In 1992, clearcuts in B.C. averaged 34.1 hectares; 32.7 hectares on the coast.

British Columbia loses $90 million annually as a result of soil erosion due to clearcutting.

Greenpeace refers to a 1988 government study to substantiate this claim, but seriously misrepresents its findings. The study in fact determined the loss of potential annual revenue resulting from productive forest land lost to road-building.

Logging roads significantly compact soils, thereby eliminating a portion of the productive forest landbase. The government study estimates that if no logging roads were built, the working forest would grow an additional $80 million worth of timber every year than it currently does.

But Greenpeace ignores the fact that our forests would generate little or no economic activity without logging roads, not to mention recreational access to many of the province's wilderness areas. This is the cost of doing business—business that generates more than $5 billion in government revenues annually.

Greenpeace also ignores the fact that many logging roads in B.C. are being 'put to bed' by processes that restore their timber-growing potential.

Many regulations

There are no laws regulating forestry in B.C.

There are six national and 20 provincial pieces of legislation regulating forestry in B.C., in addition to 700 federal and provincial regulations and over 3,000 guidelines. B.C.'s legislature enacted a comprehensive Forest Practices Code to strengthen environmental protection and monitoring, and enshrine the broad spectrum of federal and provincial laws under a single, enforceable Act.

The government of B.C. prosecuted the protesters arrested for blockading logging roads in Clayoquot Sound on behalf of [Canadian logging company] MacMillan Bloedel because they are the largest single shareholder in MacMillan Bloedel.

The provincial government did not prosecute protesters arrested in Clayoquot Sound, rather the Crown did. Those arrested on the Kennedy Lake Bridge in the summer of 1993 violated a B.C. Supreme Court injunction, and were charged with criminal contempt rather than civil contempt.

MacMillan Bloedel could not prosecute for criminal contempt. That responsibility falls to the Crown prosecutor, who operates independent of any government in Canada.

Nor was the provincial government at any time the 'largest single shareholder in MacMillan Bloedel.' The province at one time purchased 3% of the company's shares through an arm's-length investment made by an autonomous branch of government. Most of these shares have since been sold.

The 20,000 hectare Megin Watershed is one of the few victories we've achieved in B.C. It's a pristine old-growth watershed that will be preserved forever as a result of 15 years of advocacy.

While the Megin Watershed in Clayoquot Sound is a pristine old-growth watershed that will be preserved forever, it was not saved by environmentalists.

The Clayoquot compromise announced in April 1993 after more than three years of negotiation was achieved cooperatively by the forest industry, the provincial government, labour, communities, native groups and other interests. The process also involved environmentalists until they withdrew their participation.

The park status afforded the 21,300 hectare Megin Watershed, and a further 66,300 hectares in Clayoquot Sound, was achieved by the British Columbians who stayed at the negotiation table and reached consensus.

Nor is the Megin the only Vancouver Island old-growth watershed to receive park status. The Upper Carmanah, the Walbran, the Tsitika, the Tahsish Kwois and 19 other old-growth reserves were dedicated in 1994.

Virtually every Vancouver Island watershed identified by environmental groups for preservation over the past decade is now dedicated park land.

Once Clayoquot Sound is logged, all of the animals in the region will be competing for habitat in the 20,000 hectares of remaining old-growth in the Megin Watershed.

This statement is untrue for several reasons.

Firstly, the Megin Watershed hardly represents the only old-growth preserved in Clayoquot Sound. Together with neighbouring Strathcona Provincial Park, the Megin is part of more than 100,000 hectares of contiguous old-growth forest forever protected from development.

Secondly, most of the animals found in the region require a variety of forest and landscape types to fulfill their habitat needs. Young second-growth forests and even recently harvested clearcuts are as important a wildlife habitat as old-growth.

Eighty years after replanting, second-growth forests will only be half as tall as old-growth forests.

This is a generalization. It may be true for some forest types and untrue for others.

Even where it is true, having a range of tree heights and ages across a forest landscape is hardly an undesirable condition. It's a feature of naturally regenerating forests that provides a diversity of wildlife habitat.

Young second-growth forests and even recently harvested clearcuts are as important a wildlife habitat as old-growth.

The provincial government could impose $1 million fines on logging companies, but refuses.

The provincial government is currently [as of May 1994] developing forestry legislation that will enable it to levy fines of up to $1 million. It does not yet have the legal ability to do so.

Ten acres is harvested every day in Clayoquot Sound.

This exaggerates the truth by some 50%. The Clayoquot compromise allows 1,000 hectares to be harvested each year in the region, or 2.7 hectares (6.7 acres) per day. Areas cut are replanted or managed for natural regeneration.

B.C. plywood is cheaper in Japan than it is in B.C.

As international markets fluctuate, this may be true on any specific day. But over the long run, the Japanese market for B.C. plywood shows a higher average return than any other.

If Greenpeace's claim was true, B.C. would be charged for dumping under existing rules for international trade.

Fifty per cent of all forestry jobs in B.C. have been lost in the past decade.

This is patently false. B.C. Stats reports 93,000 British Columbians were employed in the forest sector in 1983. By 1993, that number had risen to 94,000.

Greenpeace bases its statement on declining union membership in the forest sector, but does not take into account growing non-union employment in value-added manufacturing, silviculture and other areas.

Clearcutting affects ocean water temperature.

False. We are unaware of any study that substantiates this claim.

Eighty-six per cent of Canadians are opposed to logging in Clayoquot Sound.

The Angus Reid poll commissioned by Greenpeace and quoted above is misrepresented. In fact, the poll suggests only 28% of Canadians are opposed to logging in Clayoquot Sound.

The poll was also biased by stating two-thirds of Clayoquot Sound would be logged. The percentage of Canadians opposed to the Clayoquot compromise could well be lower if the forest area to be logged was correctly represented as 40%.

More and more loggers are blockading logging roads in B.C.

No evidence is offered to substantiate the claim that loggers blockading logging roads is a growing trend.

In fact, a MarkTrend poll indicates the public approval rating of environmental groups has plummeted to a five-year low, largely because of road blockades during the summer of 1993. In less than a year and a half, the percentage of British Columbians who characterized the environmental movement as 'very' or 'quite responsible' has plummeted from 79% to 51%. Forest companies have a higher approval rating among British Columbians (56%) than environmentalists who blockade logging roads.

Only three different tree species are planted in B.C. forests.

Greenpeace has softened its earlier claim that only monoculture tree farms are planted in B.C. by admitting three different tree species are planted. In fact, a total of 19 different species are planted in British Columbia in silviculture prescriptions designed to produce a second-growth forest with the same species mix as the one that existed before harvesting.

The Nuu-chah-nulth

British Columbians distributed small-pox infected blankets to the Nuu-chah-nulth people in Clayoquot Sound, but now practice a more subtle form of genocide.

Although the Nuu-chah-nulth population declined significantly due to the introduction of small-pox to North America, accusations of germ warfare are purely inflammatory. Anecdotal reports of the British army sending small-pox infected blankets to natives in Central Canada in the 1700s is part of Canadian history, but the practice is not documented on the West Coast. What's worse, no historical context is provided when this statement is made.

The Nuu-chah-nulth people in Clayoquot Sound are opposed to clearcut logging.

A written or spoken declaration from the Nuu-chah-nulth Tribal Council (NTC) expressing its opposition to clearcut logging does not exist. While it's possible that individuals have expressed their personal opposition, the NTC has not taken a formal position on clearcutting.

The B.C. government's agreement with the Nuu-chah-nulth people does not provide them a veto over land-use decisions in Clayoquot Sound.

The March 19, 1994, interim agreement puts all land-use decisions for the Clayoquot region in the hands of a joint management board comprised of five native and five government representatives. Any plans for logging or road-building must have the approval of not only a majority of the board, but also a majority of its native members. Although the agreement does not use the word 'veto', it clearly and explicitly provides the Nuu-chah-nulth a controlling say over any decision affecting their land.

Logging in Clayoquot Sound is accelerating. Clearcuts are getting bigger.

Logging in the Sound is declining. Allowable annual cut in the Clayoquot region decreased from 900,000 cubic meters to less than 500,000 cubic meters in 1993.

Nor are clearcuts getting bigger. In 1993, the average cutblock in Clayoquot Sound measured 13 hectares—three times smaller than the law allows.

Logging roads in British Columbia are often as wide as highways.

A two-lane highway in B.C. is generally 66-feet wide. A few permanent mainline logging roads in B.C. may approach 30 feet in width, but most spur roads are no wider than 15 feet.

Logging in [Clayoquot] Sound is declining.

The government of B.C. has adopted the low end of the Brundtland Report by setting a goal of 12% protection for its representative eco-systems. Brundtland recommends up to 24% protection.

The 1987 United Nations Brundtland Report, entitled *Our Common Future*, recommends countries around the world strive to protect 12% of their representative eco-systems. The British Columbian government has adopted Brundtland's 12% principle as a goal to be achieved by the end of the 1990s.

But 12% is by no means the low-end, or minimum goal, recommended by the Brundtland Commission. Twenty-four per cent is never mentioned.

Clearcutting damages soil irreversibly.

Clearcutting does not damage soil irreversibly. If practised properly, it doesn't damage soil at all.

This fact is borne out by the 87% survival rate of seedlings planted in clearcut areas of British Columbia. Irreversibly damaged soil could not return such impressive results.

Prime Minister Jean Chretien has expressed his opposition to clearcut logging in B.C.

He has not.

Six young Roosevelt elk found dead at the side of a logging road on Vancouver Island were killed by loggers.

While the carcasses of six young Roosevelt elk were indeed found by the side of a logging road on Vancouver Island, the poachers have not been caught. To claim loggers are responsible is inflammatory.

B.C. is ignoring Canada's commitment to the Biodiversity Convention and Forest Principles agreed upon at the Earth Summit in 1992.

B.C. is in no way contravening the Convention on Biological Diversity or the Forest Principles agreed to in Rio [de Janeiro] by harvesting its temperate rainforests. Nor could Greenpeace provide any evidence to support its claim. With 8.4 million hectares of ancient temperate rainforest remaining, a Protected Areas Strategy that has as its goal the protection of 12% of representative eco-systems, and millions of hectares of old-growth that will never be logged for geographic reasons, the biodiversity contained in B.C.'s temperate rainforests is far from threatened.

By promoting an international boycott of B.C. forest products, Greenpeace itself is ignoring international agreements reached at the Earth Summit. Agenda 21 of the Rio Declaration clearly opposes the use of economic and trade instruments to bring about changes in environmental practice.

Despite widespread calls for the whole area to be protected, for example as a U.N. Biosphere Reserve . . . a land use plan for Clayoquot Sound was published in April 1993 that allows logging in all but 26% of the Sound's original pristine forests.

The latter portion of this statement—that only 26% of the Sound's forests won't be logged—has been addressed earlier. In fact, 60% will never be logged.

Greenpeace's recommendation that Clayoquot Sound be considered for U.N. Biosphere Reserve status is an interesting one. It has been suggested as a likely candidate because the current land use plan is a model of sustainable development, balancing conservation with human economic activities. Sustainable development is the guiding principle for U.N. Biosphere Reserves, not outright protection from resource extraction as Greenpeace believes.

(Vancouver Island marmots') natural behaviour has been dramatically altered by clearcut logging. Almost half the population has moved into clearcuts— a change that has disrupted natural migration and breeding patterns and exposed the animals to more severe weather conditions.

The marmot is not a temperate rainforest species. It is typically found in sub-alpine meadows, although colonies have recently established in upper elevation clearcuts.

The assertion that marmots living in clearcuts suffer disrupted breeding patterns and exposure to severe weather conditions is unsubstantiated. Individuals living in clearcuts have a shorter life expectancy than those in natural meadows, however, likely as a result of increased predation.

Protecting animals

Forage-dependent species like Roosevelt elk and blacktail deer rely on uncut forest for protection from predators such as wolves.

Elk and deer do use old-growth stands for cover, but they also use stands of much younger age. In fact, the forest that provides the best security cover for such species may well be dense regenerating stands of conifers. Ungulates also rely on the lichen present in old-growth forests as a food source in winter. To address this need, many logging companies maintain elk and deer winter ranges by managing second-growth stands to exhibit old-growth characteristics.

It should also be noted that elk and deer rely on open areas for forage, and make extensive use of logged areas for feeding.

Roosevelt elk are an old-growth dependent species which has lost 94% of its habitat to logging.

Roosevelt elk is not an old-growth dependent species. One of its habitat requirements is winter cover, which old-growth forests can provide, but much younger forests fulfill this need as well.

Forest land is managed in British Columbia to ensure that this and other habitat requirements are addressed.

The suggestion that 94% of the Roosevelt elk's habitat has been lost to logging is peculiar. Even if one assumes this refers to old-growth forest, about 80% of B.C.'s original old-growth remains intact.

The truth is the wolf population on Vancouver Island is as healthy as ever, partly because of logging.

In Clayoquot Sound, wolf packs range in size from 2 to 11 individuals. The breaking up of packs through forest fragmentation may disrupt behaviour that is critical to their survival.

Wolf packs are governed by the availability of food, and will roam across many habitat areas in search of deer, elk and other prey. Packs will separate and re-congregate at different times of the year, but no evidence exists to suggest forest fragmentation results in smaller packs.

In addition, this statement is at odds with a previous one. If forest fragmentation renders deer and elk more vulnerable to predators, as Greenpeace claims, why would it reduce the size of wolf packs?

The truth is the wolf population on Vancouver Island is as healthy as ever, partly because of logging. The creation of new open spaces has provided more forage for deer, elk and other species, increasing their number and the available prey for wolves.

Bird populations are three times as dense in old-growth forests as in second-growth forests.

No sources are cited, and we are unaware of any study that supports this statistic.

Three-quarters of the species in B.C.'s coastal temperate rainforest have never been documented.

The accuracy of this statement is doubtful, since we cannot possibly know how many species we do not yet know.

But the point is a good one; that enough temperate rainforest must be preserved to protect biodiversity. This is precisely why British Columbia is committed to preserving 12% of its representative eco-systems by the end of the 1990s.

Dire consequences of clearcutting include: landslides, soil erosion, debris and sediment wash into streams, leaching of nutrients from soils, flooding, loss of fish habitat, clogging of shellfish beds, alteration of river ecology, increased fire risk, forest and wildlife fragmentation, removal of vital standing and fallen dead trees, loss of shelter and food for animals, wildlife killed by machinery, loss of genetic diversity, and extinction of wildlife species.

While many of these consequences may result from logging activity, none are inevitably linked to the practice of clearcutting. Managed properly, none of these effects need occur.

B.C.'s Forest Practices Code is intended to address all of the negative effects of poor logging practices, and reduce or eliminate the environmental damage caused by forestry operations.

Greenpeace has been very successful in associating in the public's mind the above-listed negative consequences with clearcutting. But clearcutting is no better or worse than any other harvesting system, except in its application.

Small clearcuts increase the amount of exposed forest edge. This leads to increased wind damage, almost always with the loss of many more trees.

Wind damage depends on a number of factors, including soil type, tree species and topography. These factors are all considered before the size and location of clearcuts are approved under the Forest Practices Code.

This line of argument has replaced Greenpeace's former arguments against large clearcuts as the size of cutblocks in B.C. continues to shrink. To state that small clearcuts result in increased wind damage reveals a superficial understanding of a complex issue.

The small patches of forest that remain in chequerboard-type logging do not provide enough habitat for those species that rely on the interior of the forest for their survival.

Chequerboard-type logging is not practised in B.C., partly because of the terrain and partly to preserve wildlife habitat. The issue of interior forest versus forest edge habitat is understood very well in our province, and forests are managed to protect appropriate amounts of each.

(Seedlings planted in clearcuts) often . . . do not establish successfully. Areas near Ucluelet, which is to the south of Clayoquot Sound, have been planted as many as three or four times without success.

The survival rate for seedlings planted in B.C. is 87%.

The law requires that in areas where reforestation fails, companies continue to practise silviculture until the new forest reaches a free-to-grow stage.

The Clayoquot region is particularly responsive to reforestation. About 1% of reforested areas in Clayoquot Sound have been planted twice. No area has been planted three or four times.

Natural regeneration is so prolific that in combination with planting it has produced densities as high as 50,000 stems per hectare—well above the norm of 1,000 stems per hectare.

Greenpeace statements originate from 1) 'Stop the Chop Canada' leaflet; 2) 'Clearcut Sound: The Impact of Logging on the Environment and Wildlife' booklet; 3) Oral presentations to the U.K. public attended by Forest Alliance representatives March–April, 1994.

10

Teak Trees Are in Ample Supply

Simon Kloos

Simon Kloos is a contributor to Asian Timber, *a monthly magazine from Singapore that covers Southeast Asia's forestry and wood processing industries.*

Teak trees—one of the most valuable sources for wood products— are a sustainable and protected rainforest resource in Asia and elsewhere. Conservation and regulations have resulted in a plentiful supply of teak grown in natural settings and on plantations. Therefore, export restrictions should be relaxed to allow greater export of sawn teak and logs.

L imited supplies, an increase in domestic demand and government export restrictions have inhibited the trade and threatens to reduce the use of teak worldwide. As a result, it is being forced out of traditional and high profile end-uses. Of the three major teak exporting countries of Myanmar, Thailand and Indonesia, only Myanmar exports sawn teak and logs. Government restrictions in Thailand and Indonesia only permit the export of manufactured goods, and here lies the roots of the problem.

Teak is used in a wide variety of end-products, including flooring, garden furniture, interior furniture, small yacht and liner construction, interior joinery, architectural and heavy construction. However, only flooring and garden furniture can easily be exported as finished goods.

The majority of teak has to be custom manufactured or fitted on site; most is purchased in small volumes by the end consumer, or is required with too short a lead time to be sourced direct from Asia. It is impossible for such items to be imported as finished products. Thailand and Indonesia have found that such broad export restrictions have also damaged their local teak markets. The domestic market requires second grade constructional material and low cost, short/narrow strips for export production of flooring and furniture.

However, the main export markets require the more expensive first quality long strips and boards. These differing domestic and export re-

From Simon Kloos, "Teak—Down but Not Out," *Asian Timber*, 1995. Reprinted by permission of *Asian Timber*, a Singapore-based magazine serving the forest, wood panels, woodworking, and furniture industries of the Asia-Pacific region.

quirements used to complement each other—the valuable sawn exports subsidising the domestic and finished product export markets. But when all sawn exports were restricted, the overall production costs had to be averaged out, dramatically increasing the price of teak in the producers' home markets—causing difficulties for producers and consumers. Thailand, a major importer of Burma teak logs, successfully implemented an ideal solution for many years. Exports of sawn teak were only permitted from certain licensed mills in lengths over six feet.

Shorter lengths and second quality went into the home market for domestic construction or furniture exports, subsidised by the export of the more expensive long strips and boards. Unfortunately, this policy was discontinued, to be replaced by a total ban on the export of sawn teak for political rather than economic reasons. At present, the main demand for sawn teak is satisfied by Myanmar, both from mills in Yangon, and from offshore mills in Singapore, Hong Kong and China, where logs imported from Yangon are converted.

Far from a bleak situation

The strain of such world demand on a restricted supply is beginning to show in higher prices, more difficult sourcing and a reduction in the volume of teak used in the traditional markets. But the outlook is not all bleak—far from it. Teak will always be in demand due to the nature of the wood and the history and tradition that surrounds it. Exceptional durability, stability, strength and its attractive appearance make teak one of the world's leading timbers, limited in use only by restricted supplies and high price. Its natural habitat is the mixed deciduous forests of Asia, an area which extends from India, through Myanmar and northern Thailand and touches Indo-China. It can also be found in plantations throughout the world.

Teak can claim to be the most environmentally protected hardwood in Asia.

The origin of teak trading is lost in time. However, documentary evidence shows that teak was traded from India into the Mediterranean and North Africa for the ship and boat building industries as far back as the seventh century. It has been widely used in India for more than 2,000 years and examples of teak can still be seen in temples dating back more than 1,000 years. When used under cover, it is virtually imperishable. Testament to teak's strength and durability is that it was considered the most suitable timber for the construction of large sailing vessels such as the China tea clippers. These vessels had an immense spread of canvas for their size and were driven hard in the effort to be the first home with the new season's tea. It was essential, therefore, that the workmanship and materials were of the best. And so it was that shipbuilding introduced teak to the West. It still remains the key timber in ship and yacht making.

Teak has always been, and still is, managed on a strict sustained yield basis, more important today than ever before, whether it be natural re-generation or plantation growth. In most countries, the exploitation of teak resources has fallen directly under government control. Although nothing is ever perfect, teak can claim to be the most environmentally protected hardwood in Asia.

The Burma heritage

There are instances of general trading between Europe and Burma as far back as the 14th century. By the 1900s, the basis of the Burma teak trade was firmly established and Burma became the principal source of teak to the world market. In 1948, Burma gained its independence. The new government held that the country's riches, including timber, should no longer be exploited by others and plans were initiated for the gradual takeover by the state of all foreign operations. The Myanmar Timber Enterprise, a state run company, currently has the total monopoly on Burma teak.

In 1856, Dr. Dietrich Brandis, a German botanist working for the government of India, arrived in Burma. Dr. Brandis' recommendations became the basis of the Forestry Policy that is still in force today. His first priority was, "to protect and, as far as possible, to improve the forests, to arrange the cutting so as to keep well within the productive power of the forests and to ensure a permanent and sustained yield from them". The Burma Forest Act of 1881, with subsequent amendments to reflect changing situations, still remains as the basic law covering forestry in Burma, now Myanmar.

Unlike Java, where teak is found in pure stands, teak trees growing naturally in the forests of Myanmar are scattered. It was therefore essential to instigate an effective forestry management system in order to maintain a sustained teak source. So, over 40 years, Dr. Brandis created the 'Burma Selection System' to meet this need. He was acutely aware of the failings of human nature. He believed that unless a forest had a long-term commercial value, it was unlikely to be protected. "Cutting, however, has to be made in order to produce money. I know perfectly well that unless the forest could be made an annual net source of revenue for the government, regular forest management was unlikely to be maintained. These cuttings, however, I was determined, should be regulated by a well considered plan, the object of which would be the maintenance and not the exhaustion of the forests," added Dr. Brandis.

Forestry officials survey the area that is to be harvested and mark and record the individual teak trees that may be cut. This is usually specified by measuring the girth of the tree at breast height to ensure that the size falls within the parameters laid down by the Burma Selection System. Extraction is slow and labour intensive. Elephants are an essential part of the teak trade. For extraction in relatively accessible areas, buffalo and bullocks can be employed. But most of the forest areas have limited infrastructure and are mountainous, crossed by numerous valleys and creeks. Using elephants, the logs can be dragged out avoiding destruction of the rest of the forest, including the younger teak trees that are not yet large enough for felling. The Forestry system in Myanmar still, and will hopefully always, ensure a continuing source of teak and of revenue for the country as envisaged by Dr Brandis. It is, however, a shame that the exports of sawn timber from Myanmar, especially in the higher value specifications, is so limited, with logs that should be converted in Myanmar being exported to the offshore mills.

Plantation teak in Java

Teak is not indigenous to Java, although conditions are favourable for its growth. Almost 700 years ago, Buddhist monks from Burma and Siam brought seeds or saplings over to Java, where teak is known by the local name of jati. These were planted around temples and palaces and later spread naturally in pure stands, unlike its habitat in Myanmar where it tends to grow in mixed forests. To this day, there remain 'natural' teak forests in Java, mostly protected.

In the 19th century, teak plantations were laid down in the east of Java, haphazardly at first, but soon a professional system was established. The oldest plantation standing in Java is about 105 years old. The Dutch were responsible for developing both the plantations and exports and placed all teak under government control. Teak remained under government control after independence and in December 1961, Perum Perhutani, a state-owned organisation, was established to take on the responsibility for all the Javanese plantations.

Even on the relatively small island of Java, wide differences in the quality of teak can be found because of varying rainfall and soil conditions. The best plantations are to the north of the mountain chain, in an area straddling the border of East and Central Java. The best quality obtainable is virtually indistinguishable from Burma teak. Perum Perhutani is responsible for about three million hectares of production and protection forest and plantations on the islands of Java and Madura, including about 650,000 hectares of teak plantation in Java. Their brief is not just to manage the forest, but also, as depicted in their logo, to be heavily involved in the health and welfare of the local population and in the development of local industries. Perhutani has been labouring to improve the quality, yield and value of the plantations and their products in a number of ways, including the establishment of seed production areas in 1981.

Perhutani has been labouring to improve the quality, yield and value of the [Javanese] plantations and their products.

Java teak has, over the past 20 years, gained a significant market share of the teak imported into Europe, mainly in scantlings specifications, i.e. strips under six inches wide. Exports of Java teak reached a peak of about 30,000m³ a year. However, to follow the Indonesian government's policy to create employment for the large and rapidly growing population of Indonesia and to promote further processed industries, in January 1991 the central government implemented a heavy export tax on sawn timber.

The new tax on teak was raised to US$500/m³, equivalent to between 40% and 100% of the FOB [free on board] value, depending on specification. In addition, lengths under six feet, which made up the bulk of the export volume, were no longer allowed for export. In June 1991, the tax was hiked up to US$1,200/m³, effectively discouraging any further sawn exports. Java teak is now exported only as further processed products, such as flooring and garden furniture. The export restrictions have been successful to a degree.

Exports of flooring and furniture have increased, but these industries cannot use all the teak produced, nor make the best of the higher valued specifications. As a result, the best return from these well run plantations is not being realised. Perhaps Thailand's previously successful formula of export of sawn teak being restricted to high value specifications is the answer?

Organizations to Contact

The editors have compiled the following list of organizations concerned with the issues debated in this book. The descriptions are derived from materials provided by the organizations. All have publications or information available for interested readers. The list was compiled on the date of publication of the present volume; names, addresses, phone and fax numbers, and e-mail and Internet addresses may change. Be aware that many organizations take several weeks or longer to respond to inquiries, so allow as much time as possible.

Canadian Nature Federation
1 Nicholas St., Suite 606
Ottawa, ON K1N 7B7
CANADA
(800) 267-4088
(613) 562-3447
e-mail: cnf@cnf.ca
Internet: http://www.magma.ca/~cnfgen

The federation seeks to protect the Canadian landscape through a two-pronged strategy of establishing protected wilderness areas and promoting ecologically sound environmental management policies. It implements several programs focusing on areas such as wildlands conservation, habitat conservation, and ancient forest protection. It publishes the magazine *Nature Canada* and the quarterly newsletter *Nature Alert*.

Canadian Pulp & Paper Association (CPPA)
1155 Metcalfe St., 19th Fl.
Montreal, PQ H3B 4T6
CANADA
(514) 866-6621
fax: (514) 861-8817
e-mail: communic@cppa.ca
Internet: http://www.portes.ouvertes.cppa.ca

The CPPA represents forest products companies across Canada. It strives to increase the knowledge base of the pulp and paper industry through research into improvement of the industry's environmental performance, maintenance of biodiversity, and sustainable forest management practices. The CPPA produces the educational projects *Discovering the Treasure: Our Forests of Today and Tomorrow* and *A Forest for All*.

Competitive Enterprise Institute (CEI)
1001 Connecticut Ave. NW, Suite 1250
Washington, DC 20036
(202) 331-1010
fax: (202) 331-0640
e-mail: info@cei.org
Internet: http://www.cei.org

The CEI encourages the use of private incentives and property rights to protect the environment. It advocates removing governmental barriers in order to establish a system in which the private sector would be responsible for the environment. CEI publications include the monthly newsletter *CEI Update,* the book *The True State of the Planet,* and the report *The World's Forests: Conflicting Signals.*

Environmental Defense Fund
257 Park Ave. South
New York, NY 10010
(212) 505-2100
fax: (212) 505-0892
Internet: http://www.edf.org

The fund is a public interest organization of lawyers, scientists, and economists dedicated to the protection and improvement of environmental quality and public health. It publishes the bimonthly *EDF Letter* and the reports *Fires in the Amazon* and *Murder, Mahogany, and Mayhem: The Tropical Timber Trade.*

Forest Alliance of British Columbia
PO Box 49312
1055 Dunsmuir St.
Vancouver, BC V7X 1L3
CANADA
(604) 685-7507
(800) 567-TREE
fax: (604) 685-5373
Internet: http://www.forest.org

The Forest Alliance is a coalition of citizens whose common concern is to protect British Columbia's forest environment and forest-based economy. Members seek to combine environmental protection with economic stability in the use of forest resources, and they work to keep the public informed of the current state of British Columbia's forests and forestry practices. The Forest Alliance's publications include the journal *Choices* and the reports *Forests on the Line* and *Tropical and Temperate Rainforests.*

Global Warming International Center (GWIC)
International Headquarters
22W381 75th St.
Naperville, IL 60565-9245
(630) 910-1551
fax: (630) 910-1561
e-mail: syshen@magsinet.net
Internet: http://www2.msstate.edu/~krreddy/glowar/glowar.html

The GWIC is an international body that disseminates information concerning global warming science and policy. It serves both governmental and nongovernmental organizations as well as industries in more than one hundred countries. The center sponsors research on global warming and its mitigation. It publishes the quarterly newsletter *World Resource Review.*

Greenpeace USA
1436 U St. NW
Washington, DC 20009
(202) 462-1177
fax: (202) 462-4507
Internet: http://www.greenpeaceusa.org

Affiliated with Greenpeace International, this organization consists of conservationists who believe that verbal protests against environmental threats are inadequate, and they instead advocate action through nonviolent confrontation. Greenpeace's many concerns include preserving biodiversity and preventing pollution. It publishes *Greenpeace Magazine* as well as books and reports, including *Principles and Guidelines for Ecologically Responsible Forest Use*.

Heritage Foundation
214 Massachusetts Ave. NE
Washington, DC 20002-4999
(202) 546-4400
fax: (202) 546-8328
Internet: http://www.heritage.org

The Heritage Foundation is a conservative think tank that supports free enterprise and limited government in environmental matters. Its publications, such as the quarterly magazine *Policy Review* and the occasional papers *Heritage Talking Points,* include studies on environmental regulations and government policies.

International Society of Tropical Foresters (ISTF)
5400 Grosvenor Ln.
Bethesda, MD 20814
(301) 897-8720
fax: (301) 897-3690
Internet: http://www.uia.org/uiademo/org/b5367.htm

The ISTF strives to develop and promote ecologically sound methods of managing and harvesting the world's tropical forests. The society provides information and technical knowledge about the effects of deforestation on agriculture, forestry, industry, and the environment. The ISTF publishes the quarterly newsletter *ISTF News*.

International Wood Products Association (IHPA)
4214 King St. West
Alexandria, VA 22302
(703) 820-6696
fax: (703) 820-8550
e-mail: info@ihpa.org
Internet: http://www.ihpa.org

The IHPA is committed to the promotion and enhancement of trade in the imported wood products industry. Through its Conservation, Utilization, Reforestation, Education (CURE) Program, the IHPA seeks to increase public acceptance and use of wood products and to illustrate the positive role commercial forestry plays in the conservation of the world's tropical forests. It publishes bulletins and the newsletter *IHPA News*.

Rainforest Action Network (RAN)
450 Sansome St., Suite 700
San Francisco, CA 94111
(415) 398-4404
fax: (415) 398-2732
e-mail: rainforest@ran.org
Internet: http://www.ran.org

RAN works to preserve the world's rainforests through activism and by addressing the logging and importation of tropical timber, cattle ranching in rainforests, and the rights of indigenous rainforest peoples. It also seeks to educate the public about the environmental effects of tropical hardwood logging. RAN's publications include the monthly bulletin *Action Report* and the semiannual *World Rainforest Report*.

Rainforest Alliance
65 Bleecker St.
New York, NY 10012
(212) 677-1900
fax: (212) 677-2187
Internet: http://www.rainforest-alliance.org

The alliance is composed of individuals concerned with the conservation of tropical forests. Its members strive to expand awareness of the role the United States plays in the fate of tropical forests and to develop and promote sound alternatives to tropical deforestation. The alliance publishes the bimonthly newsletter *Canopy*.

Rainforest Conservation Fund
2038 N. Clark St.
Chicago, IL 60614
e-mail: rcf@interaccess.com
Internet: http://homepage.interaccess.com/~rcf

The Rainforest Conservation Fund is a volunteer organization dedicated to preserving the world's tropical forests. Its main project focuses on the rainforest preserve Reserva Comunal Tamshiyacu-Tahuayo in the Peruvian Amazon. The fund works with the local people to develop preservation programs and to maintain the integrity of the forest. Articles and field reports published by the fund include *The Importance of Blackwater Rivers as an Ecosystem* and *Why the Tahuayo River?*

Reason Foundation
3415 S. Sepulveda Blvd., Suite 400
Los Angeles, CA 90034-6064
(310) 391-2245
fax: (310) 391-4395
e-mail: cato@ix.netcom.com
Internet: http://www.reason.org

The Reason Foundation is a national public policy research organization. It specializes in a variety of policy areas, including the environment, education, and privatization. The foundation publishes the monthly magazine *Reason* and the book *Global Warming: The Greenhouse, Whitehouse, and Poorhouse Effect*.

Sierra Club
85 Second St., 2nd Fl.
San Francisco, CA 94105
(415) 977-5500
e-mail: activist-desk@sierraclub.org
Internet: http://www.sierraclub.org

The Sierra Club is a grassroots organization that promotes the protection and conservation of natural resources. It publishes the bimonthly magazine *Sierra,* the monthly Sierra Club activist resource the *Planet,* and several books, including *Into the Amazon: The Struggle for the Rainforest* and *Lessons of the Rainforest.*

World Resources Institute (WRI)
1709 New York Ave. NW
Washington, DC 20006
(202) 638-6300
fax: (202) 638-0036
e-mail: lauralee@wri.org
Internet: http://www.wri.org

The WRI conducts policy research on global resources and environmental conditions. It publishes books, reports, and papers; holds briefings, seminars, and conferences; and provides the print and broadcast media with new perspectives and background materials on environmental issues. The institute publishes the books *The Right Climate for Carbon Taxes: Creating Economic Incentives to Protect the Atmosphere* and *The Greenhouse Trap: What We're Doing to the Atmosphere and How We Can Slow Global Warming.*

Worldwatch Institute
1776 Massachusetts Ave. NW
Washington, DC 20036-1904
(202) 452-1999
fax: (202) 296-7365
e-mail: worldwatch@worldwatch.org
Internet: http://www.worldwatch.org

Worldwatch is a research organization that analyzes and focuses attention on global problems, including environmental concerns such as maintaining biodiversity and the relationship between trade and the environment. It compiles the annual *State of the World* anthology and publishes the bimonthly magazine *World Watch* and the *Worldwatch Paper Series,* which includes *Saving the Forest: What Will It Take?* and *Reforesting the Earth.*

Bibliography

Books

Dennis T. Avery	*Saving the Planet with Pesticides and Plastic.* Indianapolis: Hudson Institute, 1995.
Michael J. Balick, Elaine Elisabetsky, and Sarah A. Laird, eds.	*Medicinal Resources of the Tropical Forest: Biodiversity and Its Importance to Human Health.* New York: Columbia University Press, 1996.
Darryl Cole-Christensen	*A Place in the Rain Forest: Settling the Costa Rican Frontier.* Austin: University of Texas Press, 1997.
J. Robert Hunter	*Simple Things Won't Save the Earth.* Austin: University of Texas Press, 1997.
C.J. Jepma	*Tropical Deforestation: A Socio-Economic Approach.* London: Earthscan, 1995.
Christopher Joyce	*Earthly Goods: Medicine-Hunting in the Rain Forest.* Boston: Little, Brown, 1994.
Ariel E. Lugo and Carol Lowe, eds.	*Tropical Forests: Management and Ecology.* New York: Springer-Verlag, 1995.
Kenton Miller and Laura Tangley	*Trees of Life: Saving Tropical Forests and Their Biological Wealth.* Boston: Beacon Press, 1993.
John Schelhas and Russell Greenberg, eds.	*Forest Patches in Tropical Landscapes.* Washington, DC: Island Press, 1996.
Thomas T. Struhsaker	*Ecology of an African Rain Forest: Logging in Kibale and the Conflict Between Conservation and Exploitation.* Gainesville: University Press of Florida, 1997.
John Vandermeer and Ivette Perfecto	*Breakfast of Biodiversity: The Truth About Rain Forest Destruction.* Oakland, CA: Food First Institute for Food and Development Policy, 1995.

Periodicals

Awake!	Special issue on rainforests, March 22, 1997. Available from Watchtower Bible and Tract Society of New York, 25 Columbia Heights, Brooklyn, NY 11201-2483.
E. Bernardes	"Bio-Piracy in the Amazon," *World Press Review*, April 1997.
Canopy	"Rainforests, Rights, and Rattan: Addressing Community Injustice in Indonesian Forest Policy," February/March 1997. Available on-line at http://www.rainforest-alliance.org.

Todd L. Capson, Phyllis D. Coley, and Thomas A. Kursar   "A New Paradigm for Drug Discovery in Tropical Rainforests," *Nature Biotechnology,* October 1996. Available from Nature America, Inc., 345 Park Ave. South, New York, NY 10010-1707.

N.R. Farnsworth   "New Drugs for the Rain Forests," *World Health,* April 1996.

Malcolm Gillis   "Tropical Deforestation: Poverty, Population, and Public Policy," *Vital Speeches of the Day,* April 1, 1996.

Randy Hayes   "The Rainforest Action Network's Founder Targets Big Timber," interview by Jim Motavalli, *E Magazine,* July/August 1997.

S.R. King and T.J. Carlson   "Transnationals with a Conscience," *Utne Reader,* March/April 1996.

T. Laman   "Borneo's Strangler Fig Trees," *National Geographic,* April 1997.

Mary Jo McConahay   "Cutting the Ends of the Earth," *Sierra,* March/April 1997.

Mary Jo McConahay   "Rainforest Logging Disrupts Deep Cultural Rhythms in Tiny Belize," *National Catholic Reporter,* December 27, 1996–January 3, 1997. Available from PO Box 419281, Kansas City, MO 64141.

Will Nixon   "Rainforest Shrimp," *Mother Jones,* March 1996.

Molly O'Meara   "Environmental Intelligence: Brazil's 'Genocide Decree,'" *World Watch,* September/October 1996. Available from 1776 Massachusetts Ave. NW, Washington, DC 20036.

Doug Peacock   "The Last Wilderness," *Outside,* August 1996. Available from PO Box 51733, Boulder, CO 80323-1733.

D.A. Schneider   "Good Wood," *Scientific American,* June 1996.

Ranil Senanayake   "Forests and Trees," *Our Planet,* vol. 7, no. 2, 1995. Available from United Nations Environment Programme, PO Box 30522, Nairobi, Kenya.

Gar Smith   "Africa's Last Rainforest," *Earth Island Journal,* Fall 1996. Available on-line at http://www.earthisland.org.

M. Tannen   "Paradise Recycled," *New York Times Magazine,* September 22, 1996.

D.A. Taylor   "Saving the Forest for the Trees: Alternative Products from Woodlands," *Environment,* January/February 1997.

C. Uhl et al.   "Natural Resource Management in the Brazilian Amazon," *BioScience,* March 1997.

Harry J. Van Buren   "Why Business Should Help Save the Rainforests," *Business and Society Review,* Fall 1995. Available from 578 Post Rd. East, Box 603, Westport, CT 06880.

Leslie Weiss   "Nigerians Risk All for Their Forests," *Earth Island Journal,* Fall 1996. Available on-line.

Index

117